THE COMMITTEE OF SLEEP

ALSO BY THE AUTHOR

The Pregnant Man and Other Tales from a Hypnotherapists's Couch

Trauma and Dreams (editor)

THE

COMMITTEE

OF SLEEP

HOW ARTISTS, SCIENTISTS, AND ATHLETES USE DREAMS FOR CREATIVE PROBLEM-SOLVING —AND HOW YOU CAN TOO

Deirdre Barrett, Ph.D.

Crown Publishers

New York

Grateful acknowledgment is made to the following for permission to reprint previously published material:

DejaNews: Quotes from rec.crafts.textiles.quilting as posted through DejaNews, www.deja.com.

Journal of Chemical Education: Excerpt from "August Kekule and the Birth of the Structural Theory of Organic Chemistry in 1858" by O. Theodore Benfey in Vol. 35, No. 1, 1958, pp. 21–23. Copyright © 1958, Division of Chemical Education, Inc. Reproduced with permission from the *Journal of Chemical Education.*

Random House, Inc., and Naomi Epel: Excerpts from WRITER'S DREAMING by Naomi Epel. Copyright © 1993 by Naomi Epel. Reprinted by permission of Carol Southern Books, a division of Random House, Inc., and the author.

San Francisco Chronicle: Quote by Jack Nicklaus from the *San Francisco Chronicle,* June 27, 1964, © *San Francisco Chronicle.* Reprinted by permission.

Morton Schatzman: Excerpts from: Morton Schatzman (1983) *New Scientist,* June 9, pp. 692–3, Morton Schatzman (1983) *New Scientist,* August 11, pp. 3–4, and Morton Schatzman (1987) *New Scientist,* December 25, pp. 36–39. Reprinted by permission.

Daryoush Tavanaipour: Excerpt from "Talk," 17th Annual International Conference of the Association for the Study of Dreams, July, 2000, Washington, D.C.

D. M. Thomas: Six lines from "House of Dreams" in SELECTED POEMS by D. M. Thomas. Used by permission of the author.

Published by Crown Publishers, New York, New York.
Member of the Crown Publishing Group.

Random House, Inc. New York, Toronto, London, Sydney, Auckland
www.randomhouse.com

CROWN is a trademark and the Crown colophon is a registered trademark of Random House, Inc.

Printed in the United States of America

Design by LEONARD W. HENDERSON

Library of Congress Cataloging-in-Publication Data
Barrett, Deirdre.
The committee of sleep : how artists, scientists, and athletes use dreams for creative problem-solving—and how you can too / Deirdre Barrett. — 1st ed.
p. cm.
1. Problem solving—Miscellanea. 2. Dreams—Case studies. 3. Dreams. I. Title.

BF1099.P75 B37 2001
154.6'3—dc21   00-059028

ISBN 0-8129-3241-2

1 3 5 7 9 10 8 6 4 2

First Edition

For my parents, John and Barbara Barrett

Contents

INTRODUCTION

Each night before retiring, the French Surrealist poet St. Paul Roux hung a sign on his bedroom door that read "Poet at work." John Steinbeck wrote, "It is a common experience that a problem difficult at night is resolved in the morning after the *committee of sleep* has worked on it." The popularity of this belief in nocturnal productivity is embodied in the cliché "Sleep on it!"

These quotes don't name the dream as spokesperson for the Committee of Sleep. However, most stories of nocturnal problem solving involve either dreams or "hypnagogic imagery"—the pictures that go through our minds as we fall asleep or slowly awaken. Laboratory research confirms what people have always known: inspiration to create, and even the answers to formal problems of logic, can indeed arrive in dreams.

In *The Committee of Sleep* I've gathered remarkable examples, historic and modern, of what dreams have brought to invention and to art. A Nobel laureate's scientific experiment, music from classical masterpieces to pop chartbusters, the occasional golf swing, innumerable novels and paintings, and two entire written languages—all of these document the contribution that the Committee of Sleep has made to our waking world.

The major concerns of dreaming are obviously our personal issues: childhood slights, current moods, and how we get along with significant others. However, these aspects of dreaming have been covered thoroughly elsewhere; essentially, all other dream books focus on them. *The Committee of Sleep* will instead examine objective problems in dreams—scientific and artistic—and what these may tell us about the nature of dreaming.

The chapters are organized by discipline, beginning with the visual arts—which reproduce natural dream imagery most closely. Later chapters describe what dreams bring to intellectual fields such as science and math. We'd all like the Committee to slip us a few prize-winning ideas, so the book will also explore how common these dreams are, who has them, and what we can do to increase their likelihood.

The idea of dream creativity is so compelling that a few bogus stories have enjoyed great tenacity in our urban folklore. In Chapter 5, devoted to the influence of dreams in the fields of science and mathematics, I'll discuss the oft-told, but never actually dreamed, origins of the models for both DNA and the atom. These stories have provoked skepticism about dream productivity. Most historical examples do check out, however, and I'll share many of these intriguing accounts in the dreamers' own words.

Some writers have glamorized dreaming as wiser than waking thought. Others characterize it as useless nonsense. The stories in *The Committee of Sleep* will demonstrate that dreaming is neither consistently wise nor consistently useless. The dream's power lies in the fact that it is so *different* a mode of thought—that it supplements and enriches what we've already done while awake.

The Committee of Sleep

I

IN THE GALLERY OF THE
NIGHT: PAINTING AND
SCULPTURE FROM DREAMS

Born in South Carolina during the Depression, Jasper Johns's artistic aspirations led him to New York, where he painted for several years without finding a unique voice. In 1954 he resolved to "stop *becoming* and *be* an artist." His inspiration was a dream in which he saw himself painting a large American flag, and the next day he began exactly that project, later titled simply *Flag*. A lengthy series of flag pictures followed, which established Johns as a major artist. His work continued with other simple, bold paintings that highlighted the design artistry of commonplace objects. He disavowed all his paintings that preceded *Flag*—destroying those still in his possession and purchasing and shredding any that came to his attention later. "Since he has never shown anything drawn before this," wrote one biographer, "the extraordinary initial impact of the image and the authority with which it is painted give the impression of a finished artist suddenly sprung from nowhere."[1] Johns later told an interviewer, "I have not dreamed of any other painting. I must be grateful for such a dream!" He laughed. "The unconscious thought was accepted by the conscious gratefully."[2]

Dreams have played a role in visual art since mankind began to represent the world. The astonishing images of the night have always inspired artists. A bird-staff and other fantastic elements, believed to represent prehistoric dreams, appear on the walls of caves in Lascaux, France. This earliest known human art, produced between 40,000 and 10,000 B.C.E., caused Pablo Picasso to exclaim, "We have invented nothing!"

Scholars know more about the strikingly similar cave art of California's Ojai Valley, or "Valley of the Moon." The earliest works found there date to 1000 A.D., but legends associated with them survived when missionaries arrived in the late 1700s. These rock paintings were done by the *'atiswinic*—a type of shaman whose title literally means "dreamer" or "having a dream." The *'atiswinic* drew fantastic animals and horned anthropomorphs set against geometric grids. We have no texts for most of the paintings and can't know exactly which ones spring from dreams. But a few were told to the missionaries as dream accounts. One of these depicts the nose of a coyote growing after he chased girls around, begging for a kiss. A second shows a man capturing the retreating sun with a stick. In yet another, a swordfish tosses a whale around, juggling his outsized adversary as though he were lighter than air.[3]

Other tribes around the world routinely use dreams as a basis for visual arts. The Chippewa of North America weave their dream images into the patterns of their banners and beadwork, and the Saroa of India paint their dreams on the walls of their houses. Australian Aborigines have long depicted the events of their Dreamtime—a complex concept that includes nocturnal dreaming—with distinctive dot paintings on bark.

In Europe there was no mandate for dream art, but artists nevertheless often portrayed nighttime visions. When religious themes dominated—and the Church was its chief patron—artists commonly depicted the great dreams of the Bible. The scriptures dictated the content; the dreams of Jacob, Mary, and Pharaoh were popular subjects. But artists conveyed the state of dreaming according to their own nocturnal world. Figures faded into mist for one, hung suspended in midair for another.

Some painted their own dreams directly. Albrecht Dürer's 1525 watercolor of a savage storm bears the following inscription:

> I saw this image in my sleep, how many great waters poured from heaven ... drowning the whole land.... The deluge fell with such frightening swiftness, wind, and roaring that when I awoke, my whole body trembled; for a long while I could not come to myself. So when I arose in the morning, I painted what I had seen.[4]

In the Romantic era, William Blake portrayed the dreams of Queen Catherine and the biblical Jacob in his distinctive mystical style, as characters soaring through the heavens. He painted his own dream as *Young Night's Thoughts* (1818), depicting himself lying on the ground dreaming, the action of the dream painted next to him, a poem based on the same dream beneath that, and finally a straightforward account of the dream.

Blake also had recurring dreams of a supernatural art instructor, with a third eye in his forehead. The instructor presented the dreaming Blake with images to paint and advised him on technique. Awake, Blake made numerous oil colors of the recommended scenes. He sketched the teacher in the straightforwardly titled *Man Who Instructed Blake in Painting in His Dreams* (1819).

The Pre-Raphaelite artist Sir Edward Burne-Jones painted romantic scenes of medieval knights and ladies dreaming about each other. Traveling to Rome by train, the artist fell asleep and dreamed so vividly of the nine muses on Mount Helicon that he felt compelled to paint them the moment he arrived at his destination. Burne-Jones wrote of this painting, *The Rose Bower* (1870–90), "I meant to depict a beautiful dream . . . in a light better than any light that ever shone . . . in a land no one can remember. . . ."[5]

Soon another artistic movement was to take dream art further than the Romantics or the Pre-Raphaelites had ever . . . well, dreamed.

THE SURREALISTS

At the end of World War I, European youth were disillusioned— none more so than young artists, who tended toward both pacifism and cynicism. They refused to spend their gifts glorifying war and the politicians who'd led millions to their deaths. Instead, a cadre of the most gifted flocked around André Breton in Paris as he called for a revolution in painting, drama, and literature.

The movement called Surrealism was to be the liberation of artistic consciousness from historical and logical constraints. As a mode of escape, Surrealists used dreams more explicitly than any school of European art before them. Breton invited the inner circle—Max Ernst, Salvador Dalí, and Man Ray—to his apartment on rue Fontaine in Paris, where they recounted their dreams to one another. Breton's *Manifesto of Surrealism* touted the "omnipotence of the dream" and described the new movement as the "resolution of the two states, dreaming and reality, which are so seemingly contradictory, into a kind of absolute reality—a surreality."[6]

Many surrealists painted specific dream images, and all of them used characteristics of the dream world such as space that has no depth or extends to infinity, and juxtaposition of incongruent objects. Salvador Dalí's *The Dream;* Max Ernst's *Dream of a Girl Chased by a Nightingale;* Paul Nash's *Landscape from a Dream;* Dalí's *The Dream Approaches;* and Gil Bruvel's *The Sleep Goes Away* are all fruits of the Surrealist dream dictation.

Surrealist cultivation of dreams found its ultimate expression with Salvador Dalí. In a delightfully eccentric volume, *Fifty Secrets of Master Craftsmanship,* Dalí dispensed advice to aspiring artists. His wisdom ranged from mundane recommendations on brush types to frequency of sexual activity (advocating celibacy while awaiting inspiration but intercourse at least daily once painting—a formula B. F. Skinner would have admired). Dalí claimed that the greatest potential inspiration lay in the dream.

"What you prevent yourself from doing and force yourself not to do, the dream will do with all the lucidity of desire," he advised. Dalí focused first on the vivid dreams that seize us just as we're beginning to fall asleep, or what psychologists call "hypnagogic imagery," with his technique of "slumber with a key." His tone was whimsical, but his intent serious as he instructed novices to sit in a comfortable armchair, "preferably Spanish":

In this posture, you must hold a heavy key which you keep suspended, delicately pressed between the extremities of the thumb and forefinger of your left hand. Under the key you will previously have placed a plate upside down on the floor. Having made these preparations, you will have merely to let yourself be progressively invaded by a serene afternoon sleep, like the spiritual drop of anisette of your soul rising in the cube of sugar of your body. The moment the key drops from your fingers, you may be sure that the noise of its fall on the upside-down plate will awaken you. . . .[7]

Dalí obtained many surreal images this way. He illustrated the essay with an example, which he called "Flesh Wheelbarrow." The twisted fibers of muscle and skin that made up this device were arrestingly bizarre even by Surrealist standards.

The Master challenged his pupils with a further claim: the premium images from sleep onset were those obtained after dining on sea urchins "gathered in the last two days that precede the full moon, choosing only those whose star is coral red and discarding the yellow." He recommended preparing them *à la Catalane,* in a chocolate-based sauce to which he also attributed psychoactive properties. Lest one think he was pulling the reader's leg, sea urchins do have a reputation as a soporific among fishermen of Creus—where they are a major harvest. Our phrase "sleeping like a log" has its equivalent there in "sleeping as though you had eaten three dozen sea urchins." One of Dalí's sketches of odd, hybrid swan-people bears the title "Dream Provoked by a Meal of Sea Urchins."

Dalí believed the elaborate nighttime dreams of REM sleep

offered more versatile images because their content could be intentionally influenced. He outlined a characteristically eccentric program of nocturnal stimulation for doing so. The final dream of the night was targeted because it was "the one closest to waking" and the only one he believed was subject to influence. Recent studies conclude that although other REM periods can be manipulated, the last one is indeed the easiest to work with. Sleep researchers who have applied tactile stimuli to the skin, played recordings of distinctive noises, or shone colored lights on subjects' closed eyes, have found that these may be incorporated into dream content. To generate a pleasing artistic image, Dalí suggested fragrance poured near the nose, soft music, or gentle pressure on the closed eyeball—all these stimuli to be provided "by one's valet."

Surrealist painters admired the new field of psychoanalysis for its emphasis on the unconscious and dreaming. The Swiss artist Peter Birkhauser, a friend of Carl Jung, filled his paintings with powerful dream images that Jung famously called "archetypes." In *The World's Wound*, Birkhauser depicted a recurring dream of a man with a terrible, bloodless, gaping split running the length of his body. The wounded man moves beseechingly toward the dreamer, struggling to speak, but always unable to do so. Years later, his canvas *Having Speech* portrayed the final version of this dream. Blood flowed from the man's wound and he was finally able to talk.

Several of Birkhauser's paintings depict death. When his wife was dying of cancer, he painted *In the Night of 13 October 1942,* based on a dream. His biographer wrote, "A miraculous being, half fish and half insect, climbed up beside Birkhauser's wife . . . From its mouth emanated a blue light. Courageously, Sibylle

Birkhauser stood still; the fish approached her as if to kiss her and she became completely illuminated by the blue light."[8] Birkhauser's last painting, completed just days before his own death, portrayed a dream in which a great, glowing beast stood over him, inspiring both awe and terror.

ARE THEY OR AREN'T THEY?

We can't simply note surreal qualities or read titles to tell which paintings began as dreams. René Magritte's *Reckless Sleeper* has been used to illustrate "dream art," but Magritte said he never used nighttime dreams in his work, and composed his paintings by an entirely rational process. Even Dalí, who derived so many paintings from his "slumber with a key" and pre-awakening stimuli, titled one painting of a sleeping woman *The Dream,* which his biographers say was closely modeled on an art nouveau pin he owned in waking life.

Frida Kahlo's painting also titled *The Dream* is another work that tempts viewers to leap nimbly to the wrong assumption. It depicts the artist, covered by vines, sleeping on a four-poster bed aloft in the sky. Above her, on the bed's canopy, lies an eight-foot skeleton, wired ominously with explosives. When I discovered this painting, I already knew that Kahlo's work had been influenced by a horrific childhood accident. Thinking it might make a good cover illustration for my earlier book *Trauma and Dreams,* I'd searched for and found an account of the picture. Kahlo described that she was sleeping peacefully in her bed and green vines grew over her. Then her bed lifted gently up and floated into the sky, pulling the vines up by their roots. End of dream. I combed other books on Kahlo for a passage explaining the skeleton's presence. Further information came in the form of another picture—this time a photograph of the artist seated on her bed under a giant papier-mâché skeleton wired with firecrackers, "a constant reminder of mortality," the legend read. She playfully referred to it as her "lover."

The dream format has also served as a convenient ruse. For years following the Communist Revolution, Russian officials forbade artists from painting anything that did not promote the Party. The art and literature of this period have been dubbed "Boy Meets Tractor." During the post-Stalin loosening of rules, other topics were again permitted, but none that were critical of the government. Symbolic art became more popular.

Painting in this era, the Russian artist Olga Bulgakoza's bold, fanciful images resembled Chagall's. Her *Dream About the Red Bird* (1989)[9] shows one man stabbing another in the back. Intermediate figures suggest they are the same man—that he ultimately kills himself. A giant red bird stands behind them. The bird's beak and claws are the same shade of yellow in the Soviet flag. The red bird casts a dark shadow over the men. Phantasmagoric dream or political allegory? We can't know whether artists working under such repressive conditions are using the structure of a dream to evade censorship, or whether the Committee of Sleep is indeed at work.

During the Soviet years, many Russians did dream thinly veiled political statements. At the time of the August 1991 coup, I was attending a dream conference in Moscow and I was among the minority of Americans who remained. Every morning the multinational group would recount their dreams. Soviets more often described politically symbolic dreams—for example, vast numbers of people being herded helplessly like cattle—while westerners presented dreams focused on their personal lives.

Although dreamlike art needn't arise from a dream, some surprisingly realistic works do. Jasper Johns's *Flag* is specifically classified by the art world as a prime example of the genre called Realism. Another American painter of the same era, Ellsworth Kelly, developed his abstract geometric assemblies of multiple canvases from a similar dream experience. Studying art in Paris under the GI Bill of Rights, Kelly was not immediately inspired in any distinctive direction. When his veteran's benefits ran out, he began teaching adolescents at the American School so he could remain in Paris.

One night Kelly dreamed he was working on a very large whirled splatter painting like the ones his sixth graders did. Still dreaming, he had the idea of cutting up the canvas and arranging the resulting sixteen pieces in a grid, with their stronger lines flowing horizontally. Kelly awoke, sketched the grid, and wrote an account ending, "In this dream is something I have been waiting for." His next painting was called *Brushstrokes Cut into 20 Squares and Arranged by Chance.* Contrary to the title's "chance," the brushstrokes are deliberately arranged horizontally as in the dream. The only change from the dream's dictation was to move from a sixteen- to a twenty-segment grid. Kelly repeated this grid theme for more than a year, and the resulting images established his reputation. One art critic observed, "What Kelly had understood through the experience of the dream and its aftermath was not just that chance could only be taken a bit at a time, but more profoundly, he understood that in order to show change, in order to make randomness visible, one had to systematize it."[10]

Lucid Dreams

Some artists have learned to dream repeatedly the kind of specific, finished works that Johns and Kelly saw. They do so intentionally by a process known as lucid dreaming.

Lucid dreams are those in which the dreamer realizes he or she is dreaming during the course of the dream. Consciousness allows the dreamer to take volitional action. Lucid dreamers may recall plans for what to do in their dreams. They carry these out even as unexpected aspects of the dream state continue to flow.

Stanford University lucidity expert Steven LaBerge devised methods to induce and shape lucid dreams.[11] LaBerge recommends asking yourself if you are dreaming during the day, and making regular checks of whether your surroundings are functioning under the waking laws of physics. This habit will eventually carry over into dreaming.

Can you take off and fly? Make a brick wall dissolve? Use your willpower to move that gorgeous stranger to embrace you? Yes? Well, you're dreaming! Can you read a long passage of text and comprehend it? Are the words still the same if you look away and then back? In the cliché of pinching yourself, do you feel immediate, realistic pain? Well, then, you're probably awake.

Artists who master lucid dreaming often use it to find inspiration for their work. For the past thirteen years, painter Epic Dewfall has used this technique to develop his canvases. "About once a month, I'll realize I'm dreaming, and when I do, I walk around in the dream looking at art on the walls. I usually find paintings on every wall. By the time one of these lucid dreams ends, I have one or two good paintings memorized." Dewfall says that most often he draws inspiration from the paintings he sees in his dream art gallery, but that a few times he has looked through pictures in a dreamed book or even rummaged through a pile of unframed art for an image to take back to the waking world.

Most lucid dreamers wish to remain in the state and enjoy a lengthy lucid dream, but sometimes the sheer excitement of knowing they are dreaming wakes them up. LaBerge suggests that novices are less likely to shake themselves out of the dream world if they avoid focusing too intently on any one object. However, when artists use this state for inspiration, waking up after examining one dramatic object is actually desirable.

"A remarkably good coincidence with getting art this way," Dewfall observes, "is that when I've found a painting I really like, I'll wake up after I have been looking at it for about six seconds. I suspect this is because I've stopped moving from painting to painting. . . . This is really more of a terrific benefit than a problem. It allows me to wake up with a very clear vision in my memory. If I were to keep lucid dreaming for another four minutes, the painting I liked so much would have disappeared from memory or at least not be so clear." [12]

NIGHTMARES AS INSPIRATION

Whether we stumble upon a horrifying scene, discover our body deteriorating in a grotesque manner, or struggle desperately to outrun a pursuer, the last line is always the same: "And then I woke up terrified." Nightmares are for many our most vivid dream experiences. Common in childhood, they're rare by adulthood, but they're still prominent in our memories. Nightmares are important for just these reasons—they wake us, ensuring our attention, and don't fade easily as we begin our day. Theorists have suggested that they are our most important dreams; Freud and Jung both paid special attention when their patients had nightmares. Pursuers of creative dreams may also be well-advised to do so. Studies have found that artists and creative people in general have more nightmares than other adults.[13]

Sculptor Penelope Jencks won a commission to cast a larger-than-life bronze statue of Eleanor Roosevelt for Riverside Park in Manhattan. The artist had almost always sculpted from live models and was anxious about doing a major project without one. She had not yet settled on an exact image of the First Lady despite collecting hundreds of photos when she had the following dream:

> I was crouched over my bicycle, which I was mending in my studio. I had heard that Eleanor Roosevelt was nearby and I was suddenly filled with elation. I realized that my problems were over, that she would pose for me and that I would be able to succeed. I cannot describe the happiness and relief that flooded through me. It was like one of those dreams that you have after losing some treasured object you love and finding it whole and back once again in your hands. I could hear a voice from outside my studio saying "Oh, here she comes." I hurried with my repairs and behind me I heard the door opening. As she entered I rose and turned to face her. She stood before me smiling, a benign, comfortable presence with a look of welcome on her face. . . . As I straightened up I saw that she towered above me. I was barely as high as her waist. My confidence shaken, I woke up in terror, realizing that I had bitten off much more than I could chew.

Both a national magazine and a scholarly book presented the dream as a direct inspiration for the art. They described the event as if Jencks had instantly awakened with her artistic block broken and sculpted the statue from the dream vision.

But when I talked to the artist, she told me emphatically that this was not the case. "No, it was a nightmare! I was terrified, overwhelmed. I thought, 'No way will you possibly be able to do this!' "

"The thing that was so horrible was that I'd had a feeling of all these options. But I'd really bitten off more than I could chew. I was not quite facing up to that fact until the dream."

So, I asked, did it help?

"No," Jencks told me. "Dreams like this have a way of forcing me to look at reality in a manner I don't ordinarily. But they don't *solve* problems—they remind me there *are* problems."

How did she eventually complete the piece? "I just gradually thought a lot about it and began to work out how I would do it." Did the finished statue look anything like the dream character of Mrs. Roosevelt? "Well, possibly," she said hesitantly. "In the dream she was fifteen or twenty feet tall—the statue is eight feet—but maybe just a little." She sounded suspicious that I might be trying to hang on to the romanticized version of the anecdote I had first read. "Mostly it was unnerving—I don't want it becoming a part of history that the dream solved it."

Jencks is not the only artist who has nightmares about her work. Some, however, report ones with a more salutary effect. The Boston painter and sculptor Paul Laffoley describes the following dream as pivotal.

"The dream began simply. I was on my way to visit an art gallery in Boston on a bright summer day. I started walking up past the Ritz Carlton without knowing how I got there but with a sense of anticipation of what I would soon see. When I came to Alpha Gallery, there was a gallery right next door called the Omega. I'd never noticed this gallery before. I thought maybe I should go in."

Laffoley moved up the imaginary gallery stairs with a slow balletic leap, and passed through the iridescent doorway. Inside, an art opening was in progress, attended by people who were unremarkable "except better dressed than was true for receptions in Boston at that time."

But what caught Laffoley's eye was the exhibit itself. Thirteen sculptures sat atop Ionic column pedestals. Each piece glowed brilliantly and created an illusion of depth beyond the few feet of real space it occupied. Laffoley recognized the technique for creating perspective and radiance as one he himself had previously employed. The secret was a light source sandwiched between multiple one- and two-way mirrors. These surreally dazzling sculptures utilized the lighting effect better than he or anyone had ever done.

They were "brilliant—both intellectually and visually," he marveled. "My first reaction was complete jealousy. Now, I normally do not feel jealous when I look at other contemporary artists' work. I may be bored, perhaps slightly interested, but not jealous. But here I was, hysterically jealous. Enraged, I stewed, 'Everything in this show has totally wiped me out! I've been absorbed. All the forms I've been thinking about or could think about for years and years to come are expressed in this work.'"

As he observed the awesome sculpture, Laffoley reported, "I was overcome with terror. . . . I knew I was trapped in the gallery and would surely die if I did not get out of this dream and out of the presence of these *sculptures*. That is when I did wake up, screaming. My bedclothes were soaked with sweat."

For several weeks, Laffoley slept as little as possible, fearing the dream would recur. But as his anxiety abated, what had seemed a curse proved a priceless gift. "I had been shown something that I could use, from which I could learn." The art that had overwhelmed him in the dream supplied the designs for his next sculptures and paintings. They carried him forward into major success as an artist. "My art began then to develop into what it is today."[14]

Long before Jencks and Laffoley, Francisco Goya sketched his frequent nightmares in his book *Los Caprichos*—including its famous frontispiece, "The Sleep of Reason Begets Monsters." *Los Caprichos* includes images of the dreamer flying, or wrestling with monsters and great birds, and scenes of sexual predation. *The Giant,* one of Goya's major oils, depicts a goliath moving over a hillside at night. His biographers believe this work, too, was based on a nightmare. In 1819, during the worst of his recurring depressions, Goya retreated from society and created what came to be known as his "Black Paintings." These were an attempt to defuse his nightmares by carefully documenting them. The Black Paintings are not as well known as "The Sleep of Reason" or *The Giant,* partly because they are judged to be of less artistic merit, and partly because Goya painted them not on canvas but on the walls of his house!

DREAM ARCHITECTURE

Architecture is a visual art, but it differs from those we've discussed in one important way. Almost anything a competent painter sees in a dream can be put on canvas. Architectural design involves engineering, and must operate within fixed structural limits. An artist can paint a building floating in air, or made of smoke, or whose paper walls hold up a lead roof—but an architect could not build it. Only a small fraction of the structures we travel through in our dreams are possible in the waking world. However, architects have translated some of these into reality.

Lucy Davis, chief architect at a major North Carolina firm, dreams many of her designs. In one example she told me about, "The dream began with a person whose outstretched arms turned into a ship with a prow pointed at the same angle. Then it became a house I was walking through. There was a section with clerestory windows; the beams crossed and created the shape of the windows."

Davis built the house in the Y shape of the person's arms and the boat's prow, and put in the windows exactly as she had seen them in the dream. "The overall plan came from the abstract part of the dream," she says. "The window details were more literally translated." The finished house received a several-page layout in an architecture magazine.[15]

"I've designed at least a dozen to fifteen houses this way." Davis says, "It typically happens when I've worked on a project but I'm not really getting anywhere. Those tend to be the ones that pop out in the dream process. I remember one house I was kind of stuck on and I had a dream that I went to a party in the finished house—that solved it! It was an incidental detail to the dream, but crucial to waking life."

Davis has always been a vivid dreamer. "When I was a child, I remembered a lot of dreams. I had sequels—I'd continue a dream from one night to the next. When I was five, I'd have these wild cartoon dreams. As an adult I don't remember so many, but the ones I have are often connected to work."

Boston architect Sang Kim recalls a dream from his student days that inspired one of his best designs. Most architectural projects begin with a walk-through of the site. But for a certain single-family housing project, Kim had merely been given information about a remote site in Georgia. "The instructor described the site as just so: lakeside, hilly, lots of trees, isolated from anything urban. Although the description of the site seemed very simple," Kim recalls, "it's a totally different experience once a person is in the actual site. It's much more than just *visual*. Although the visual is the most practical and critical element, it's only a fraction of the full experience.

"The dream occurred at a very early stage of the project," he told me. "I hadn't even begun to design the actual building. During the dream, I was walking through the site, as I would do for most of my design sites. In the dream I wasn't thinking about my design—I probably wasn't even aware of the fact that I was supposed to build something on the site. The walk-through was very real and clearly remembered. It inspired me to a particular distinctive design. If I hadn't experienced the dream, my final design would have taken a different direction, and definitely one of much less magnitude."

Many readers know that Samuel Taylor Coleridge reported that he dreamed his poem "Kubla Khan" in an opium-induced sleep, and we'll discuss this more in Chapter Three. Less well publicized is how the real palace of the ruler came to be constructed. History records that Khan himself dreamed the site and design of the "stately pleasure dome." Coleridge read a description of its construction before he fell asleep, but not one that told of its dream origin; no one translated this into English until years after Coleridge's dream. The events are eerily similar, but related only by coincidence.

Khan dreamed of a grand yet delicate palace on a sloping cliff by a deep chasm and river. He was so determined to bring this vision to life that he sent emissaries to find a site that matched the dreamed setting. Even before they located it, he sketched the design for his builders. When the searchers spotted the appropriate hill, Khan's domed palace was erected just as he had dreamed it.

Jungian analyst Cordy Fergus is a modern-day Kubla Khan. Fergus owned a tract of wooded land in Washington State with a salmon stream running through it. He pondered what sort of house to build during the same time his analytic studies dictated that he record and sketch his dreams. One night, Fergus dreamed of a Buddha-like figure meditating in a lotus position. "In that dream," he says, "the person morphed into a house." Fergus was so stuck by the image that he sketched his "Buddha house" from every angle and searched out an unconventional architect/builder, Ray Kelly, to undertake the project. Kelly improvised the three-story stucco house with huge, curved beams that had been discarded by conventional logging operations for their irregularities. The first floor consisted of two diagonal wings corresponding to the Buddha's folded legs. The middle story, or torso, contained the main living area, dominated by a massive fireplace constructed from smooth river stones. The third story, representing the head, consisted of a domed cupola with a chakra-like skylight. Fergus, himself an artist, inlaid the entryway with a mosaic Buddha made of pebbles and beach glass, to depict the first half of his dream. This spectacular creation of the Committee was recently featured on cable television's Home and Garden Channel.[16]

Just as with painting, dream-inspired buildings may be quite conventional and the most surreal architecture does not necessarily spring from dreams. Nor, again, can the names of buildings be relied on to reveal their origin. The leading tourist attraction in the French province of Drôme is a structure that an untrained postman, Ferdinand Cheval, carved into a rock hillside during approximately 93,000 of his off-duty hours over thirty-three years. Completed in 1912, the Dream Palace winds irregularly over thirty yards, studded with fantastic animals and ornate arched corridors. A jumble of styles and the influences of many cultures found their way into Cheval's creation. Years later, Picasso and Breton described the palace as the architectural expression of the Surrealist movement. André Malraux, France's minister of culture, listed the palace as a historic monument. It has been mentioned in chapters on dream art as a dream creation, and there are even quotes from Cheval translated as, "I dreamed of this palace for years before beginning it," and "I first saw the palace in my dreams." However, the French use the word *reve* just as we use the word *dream,* to denote both sleeping hallucinations and daytime goals. Cheval's longer descriptions of the palace's design indicate it is the result of the latter. He makes it clear that he first got the idea when looking at a misaddressed book on Moorish architecture that had been returned to his post office as undeliverable. He imagined further details and searched for an appropriate location while making his daily rounds for years before beginning construction of the dreamlike, but not dreamed, structure.[17]

Other Dream Designs

The camera, with its obvious real-life constraints, may not seem like a tool of the Committee. But many Surrealist artists tried their hand at representing dreams in still photography. Most used darkroom manipulation, such as double exposure, or collage, to suggest their dreamscape.

Some dreams are remarkably realistic in their imagery, and are more readily captured on film. When the director of Doubleday Press's art department, Alex Gotfryd, had a memorable dream of trailing three figures through the mist-shrouded, dawn streets of Venice, he hired three models and set off to capture his experience on film. The resulting book of photographs, *Appointment in Venice,* received wide acclaim.[18]

Author Janet Baylis interviewed applied visual artists ranging from clothing designers to interior decorators, and found that many of them reported dreaming solutions when they were stuck on projects. Some were directly presented with the final creation from the Committee one designer dreamt of herself modeling a dream dress and crying "Look! Look!" as if she wanted to call the waking ego's attention to it. Others' dreams were more abstract, like the interior decorator who found herself viewing window displays that showed how each client's personality should be expressed in differing colors and amounts of lighting. The following example contained an interesting twist in the presentation of the solution:

> I was asked to make a wedding dress for a girl that was pregnant. She was very cute and petite, but was begin-

ning to "show." I had to come up with a design that would hide her condition. I tried several ideas but none of them satisfied me or her.

One morning, out of the blue, I just woke up with the idea that I instantly drew on paper and I began to work on it. I wanted to trim it with dried flowers and make a crown of the same for the headpiece. The fabric was a Georgette sheer off-white.... When I finished it, I was very pleased and so was the bride. That night I had this dream:

A girl with no face came to thank me for making her dress over again. She never got to wear it for her own wedding because she died before the day. She was wearing exactly the same dress in my dream and said she told me how to make it. I said no, that it was my own idea, but she kept insisting she "came over" (from the other side of life) to tell me what she wanted, and I just followed instructions. She even asked, "When have you ever heard of dried flowers on a dress?" She said they were fresh when she had it.[19]

The designer came to believe she'd had a previous dream and awakened remembering only the instructions, but whether this was correct or not, it seems to have been some machination of the Committee of Sleep.

One major garden has been based largely around dreams. The Chanticleer Garden near Philadelphia was designed by landscape architect Chris Woods. One night he dreamed that the garden's oaks—already in place in waking reality—had dropped impossibly enormous acorns on the lawn. Awake, he liked the image and commissioned garden statuary to reproduce the dream. Elsewhere in the garden, stone faces from another dream stare out at visitors.[20]

Potter Anna Marie Gundlach found over time that she could design pots by waiting to see the next one in a dream. She observed the pot's shape and size; it would usually be embedded with everyday objects such as nails and fabric, and she would faithfully re-create it. This became so reliable a source of design that her major traveling show was titled "Dreams in Clay."[21]

Although Blake dreamed about instruction in painting, and Laffoley dreamed of an obscure lighting effect, these design and architectural examples stray further from the usual content of dreaming. They provide specific guidance and have a tendency to occur when the dreamer is "stuck" on a particular problem. Architecture and design can be seen as intermediate between the visual arts and other areas of creativity in the progression away from simple imagery. The disciplines in subsequent chapters call on more abstract reasoning—yet the Committee of Sleep often responds.

2

DREAMS THAT MONEY
CAN BUY: FILMMAKING
AND THEATER

*A film is not a dream that is told, but one that we all
dream together.*

JEAN COCTEAU[1]

Dreams and film have an obvious affinity: the movie theater is
as close as we may ever get to watching another person's dreams
or sharing such a private experience with an entire audience. In
Britain, the first buildings constructed for the showing of films
were referred to as "dream palaces."

> The darkness of the hall, the silent shadow gliding across
> the luminous screen—everything conspires to plunge us
> into a dreamlike state in which the suggestive powers of
> the forms playing before us become as imperious as the
> power of the images appearing in our nocturnal sleep.
> Next morning, the incoherence of the dream can make us
> smile, while it seems amazing that we could have ever

lent ourselves to such absurd adventures. Filmgoers experience similar emotions. They become the play-things of illusion, transported by a sequence of unpredictable actions or irresistible visual currents.[2]

The above words were written by silent filmmaker René Clair in 1926, but they are equally applicable today. One modern film critic suggests that filmgoers experience "bi-presence" much like a dreamer who is both actor and spectator in the dream.[3] Another observes that the "willing suspension of disbelief," Coleridge's term for the reader's readiness to accept the fictional world, "is stronger in cinema than in any other of the arts."[4]

The very act of filming adds to the dreaminess. The camera's smooth glide mimics the movement of our dreams, in which we're rarely aware of discrete steps. Even in René Clair's day, discontinuous "jump cuts" in editing suggested the sudden scene shifts in dream time and space. Objects, characters, and settings are strangely juxtaposed, but the photographic realism is so powerful that for a time we accept the most illogical events and incongruously connected facts as "real." Modern photographic techniques such as lens distortion, oblique angles, flickering, overlapping, dissolves, multiple exposures—and state-of-the-art, makeup and computer animation—make bizarre content look even more real.

Just as in the other visual arts, some films are representations of the actual nocturnal dreams of their individual filmmaker—scenes dreamed by the screenwriter or director, or characterizations that occurred to actors in their dreams. When 108 attendees at the Sundance Institute for Filmmaking were asked whether they used their dreams in their work, a majority of writers, directors, and actors said that they did—many quite often. Producers, editors, and cinematographers did so somewhat less frequently, but still more often than the general public. Writers, directors, and actors also had more nightmares than most people, they recalled more dreams generally, and they placed a higher value on the use of dreams in understanding themselves and solving personal problems.[5]

The realm of film allows not only vivid imagery but also the other key element of dreaming: the narrative, albeit a sometimes bizarre narrative. When the main creative problem is "What shall I make a movie about?" the typical production of the Committee of Sleep can more easily be viewed as containing an acceptable answer than when, as in later chapters, one is asking, "What is the structure of benzene?" "What does this Assyrian hieroglyphic say?" or "How could we manufacture insulin for diabetics?" Dreams are, essentially, an inexhaustible resource for the filmmaker awaiting a visual scene or events to complete the script.

EARLY EXPERIMENTS IN FILMING DREAMS: THE SURREALISTS

The medium of film developed at the same point in history as the movement in art that was most directly suited to using a typical dream in its unaltered form—so dreams found a natural outlet in Surrealist film.

The first dream-inspired film was the classic short *Un Chien Andalou* (1929), a collaboration between painter Salvador Dalí and a rising young director, Luis Buñuel. As Buñuel described the venture, "I told him about a dream I'd had in which a long, tapering cloud sliced the moon in half, like a razor blade slicing through an eye. Dalí immediately told me that he'd seen a hand crawling with ants in a dream he'd had the previous night. 'And what if we started right there and made a film?' he wondered aloud. . . . The script was built around those two dreams."[6]

Alfred Hitchcock later employed Dalí as a consultant for the dream sequence in his 1945 film *Spellbound*. Much of the content was dictated by the film's plot; the dream was to symbolize the amnesiac protagonist's visit to "Gabriel Valley," with imagery of him running downhill as wings flapped overhead. But Dalí designed sharply angled sets inspired by his own dream space, and inserted the same eye-cutting scene that Buñuel had dreamed. The original footage also used Dalí's favorite dream, but Hitchcock omitted the resulting scene, which would have shown Ingrid Bergman covered with ants! Dalí fell out with Hitchcock, and returned to the medium of painting, where he had total artistic control.[7]

Buñuel continued his career in film, directing such classics as *Belle de Jour* and *The Discreet Charm of the Bourgeoisie*. "I brought dreams directly into my films," he remembers. " 'Don't worry if the movie's too short,' I once told a Mexican producer. 'I'll just put in a dream.' He was not impressed."

A classic anxiety dream that recurs for many of us long after completing our studies is of arriving at an exam unprepared. Buñuel suffered from a variation common among theater folk, in which he would suddenly realize that he must go on stage in just a few minutes and play a role he hasn't learned. He reproduced these images—his dream alterego trying to postpone the performance as the impatient audience begins to hiss—in *The Discreet Charm of the Bourgeoisie*. In *The Milky Way,* the Virgin

Mary appears and uses the same words she spoke to Buñuel, an avowed atheist, in another dream.

Buñuel stated that his single favorite thing about film is that it is "the superior way of expressing the world of dreams. If someone were to tell me I had twenty years left, and ask me how I'd like to spend them," he insists, "I'd reply, 'Give me two hours a day of activity, and I'll take the other twenty-two in dreams. . . .' "[8]

Another Surrealist project, *Dreams that Money Can Buy* (1947), was the first feature-length, avant-garde film produced in America. It may have boasted the richest collection of artistic talent ever brought together on one project. Paul Bowles wrote the dialogue and a young John Cage composed the score. Surrealists, including Max Ernst, Alexander Calder, Man Ray, and Marcel Duchamps, each designed a sequence from his own dreams. In the film, a struggling artist discovers he can look into anyone's eyes and cause them to sink into a deep sleep in which they will have a "big" dream. He leases an office, fills it with a couch, surreal art, and a bust of Morpheus, the Greek god of dreams, and goes into private practice. Clients enter through one door from the waking world/waiting room. After hearing their life story, the artist opens a second door, which leads them into their dream.

Ernst's opening sequence was based on the same dream as his famous painting *Girl Menaced by a Nightingale.* The dream's suggestion of perfectly ordinary objects being unbearably sinister, only half-realized on canvas, is powerfully reproduced in the moving, changing medium of film. Without modern special effects, Ernst used choreography, sleight of hand, and surreal sets to capture the dreamlike quality of content and transitions. Tight camera angles evoke claustrophobia, and a bird trapped in a bedroom becomes utterly terrifying. At one point a red velvet curtain behind the girl trapped with the nightingale transforms abruptly into her dress, and viewers feel they are actually in Ernst's dream.

In Hans Richter's sequence, a man stops himself from committing a murder, yet finds a bloody knife in his hand. It drips more and more blood as he tries to clean it. When he grabs people, imploring them to help, their limbs fall off where he touches them. The body of one opens up to reveal a Magritte-style birdcage as his midsection. Richter masterfully captures the chaos and growing horror of a nightmare.

FROM BERGMAN TO SAYLES: DREAMS IN MODERN INDEPENDENT CINEMA

Following the Surrealists, many filmmakers have continued to use their dreams in their films, most often simply inserting them as belonging to one of their characters. "Twice I have transferred dreams to film exactly as I had dreamed them," reported the Swedish director Ingmar Bergman. "One is *Wild Strawberries,* the sequence with the coffin. Without any translation, it's just put in as it occurred in my dream."

In the scene, the protagonist, Professor Borg, walks through a deserted city street. Gazing up at a clock, he sees that its hands are missing. His brow furrows as he discovers his own watch has none, either. We hear a beating heart. Borg spots a man standing with his back turned, and reaches out to touch him. The figure turns, revealing a faceless head, and shrivels into a pile of wet, oozing rags. A hearse appears and one wheel flies loose, narrowly missing Borg. A coffin slides out and crashes onto the street. Borg approaches and leans over the smashed coffin. A hand reaches out from it and seizes him. The corpse stares up mockingly. The face is Borg's own.

The entire sequence was shot in a harsh glare of light. "My cruelest dreams are flooded with unbearable sunlight,"[9] observed Bergman. This is unusual; others' nightmares occur more often in dark settings.

Another dream, of four women in mourning, evolved into Bergman's 1972 film *Cries and Whispers*. The opening sequence of *The Naked Night,* featuring a clown and his wife, was also dreamed by Bergman. So were several images in *The Hour of the Wolf,* including a murdered boy sinking beneath the dark surface of the water. That film was named for the Swedish folk term for the hour before dawn, in which the most human deaths occur— and the most nightmares.

Other major directors have regularly inserted their dreams into films. Federico Fellini's most memorable childhood dream, of a mysterious magician, is reproduced as the finale of his film *8 1/2.*[10] Orson Welles said of *The Trial,* "I attempted to make a picture like a dream I have had. . . . I move from architecture to architecture in my dreams." When asked if the film was the character K's dream—because it began with K opening his eyes— Welles replied, "No, it's my dream. I dreamed about him."[11]

"Man is a genius while dreaming," said the Japanese director Akira Kurosawa. "Fearless and brave, like a genius."[12] One of the few films designed entirely by the Committee of Sleep is Kurosawa's *Dreams.* It consists of eight sequences, each a meticulous reproduction of one of Kurosawa's own dreams, beginning with ones he had in childhood. In the first, the young Kurosawa steals under a rainbow and into the woods to witness the wedding dance of the foxes, said to occur only when sun and rain mingle.

In the next, he searches for his lost sister and encounters a troupe of ornately costumed human *shina* dolls, who are angry that his family has felled all the trees in a peach orchard. One midlife segment features a meeting with Vincent van Gogh (played by the American director Martin Scorsese) in a landscape that looks like the painter's fantastic field of sunflowers.

In a post-traumatic nightmare, a platoon, killed in action, comes marching back to Kurosawa; he has the horrific task of telling them they are dead and ordering them into oblivion. As an elderly dreamer, he is part of a climbing party that perishes in a blinding blizzard. His role is merely that of an observer in a dream of nuclear explosions and postapocalyptic demons writhing in agony. In the final sequence, Kurosawa wanders into a small village of water mills, where a traditional Japanese funeral is in progress. He doffs his hat in respect, says good-bye, and heads off utterly alone.

Many directors film dream sequences in silence, denoting their overwhelming visual nature. Kurosawa, as Bergman did with the spooky heartbeat of *Wild Strawberries,* omitted dialogue but emphasized sounds crucial to his dreams. The moaning wind and labored breathing of exhausted explorers in the blizzard sequence are haunting, as is the approaching tramp of marching feet when the ghost platoon emerges from a dark tunnel. We get not only the content of the dreams but also a sense of what the director's dream world *feels* like.

Other screenwriters make use of suggestions from the Committee of Sleep without designating them as dreams within the film. Robert Altman made an entire film exactly as the story had unfolded in one long dream, but he chose to place the action in the waking world. *Three Women* (1977) stars Sissy Spacek as a naïve young woman who arrives in California and quickly idealizes her hyperconventional roommate, whose decor, meals, and philosophy are straight out of the apartment's abundant supply of women's magazines. Spacek is also intrigued by their mute landlady, who spends her days painting orgies of anthropomorphic mandrill baboons on the bottoms of the town's swimming pools.

Water imagery is everywhere in the film, from the nursing home where Spacek leads the infirm around a Jacuzzi for aquatherapeutics, to the lasciviously decorated pools. Many scenes begin in one watery setting and transform seamlessly to another. Characters morph fluidly into one another. The first identity switch occurs when Spacek nearly drowns in the apartment swimming pool and wakes up insisting she is her roommate. Soon the women are swapping identities without the benefit of logical plot devices. They become increasingly indistinguishable until the landlady, who has not yet spoken a word, comes to tell the others that she has just had "the most wonderful dream." On that cue, the closing credits roll.[13]

Three Women received excellent reviews, but turned in one of Altman's worst box-office performances ever—possibly because he used the dream in such a raw form, far removed from the average viewer's conventions about storylines.

Other filmmakers rework dream material radically before filming it. Director/writer/actor John Sayles had three dreams over the course of a week, which he combined to produce his comedy *The Brother from Another Planet*. Sayles describes this sequence in Naomi Epel's book *Writers Dreaming*.

On the first night, he dreamed that he had been hired to write the script for a film that had already begun shooting (in typical dream logic!). He was watching the completed scenes on a screen. "The name of the movie was *Assholes from Outer Space,*" Sayles recalls. "I saw the title coming at me in 3–D—streaking at me like in a fifties science fiction movie—*Assholes from Outer Space!* With tinny music. And then a really lame fifties scene from something like *Reefer Madness.* It was about these people who look just like us—with kind of fifties suits on—but they had antennas in their heads. They were like bureaucrats who worked in motor vehicle departments and banks. And they were assholes."

Sayles awoke amused by the dream, but it seemed to him more like a skit than a film script. A couple of nights later he dreamed that he had been hired to direct a half-completed movie. This oneiric film, titled *Bigfoot in the City,* was about a yeti who had accidentally wandered into a metropolis. The most vivid scene was of two cops cornering the yeti in an alleyway. They stood over the wounded and bleeding creature, sympathetic, but baffled as to what to do, so one cop finally said to the other, "Book him." Sayles's association was that the dream was "very much like this Carol Reed film where there's an IRA guy who's on the run because he was in a shootout and the cops are after him—except he's a Bigfoot instead of a real person."

This dream appealed to Sayles as dramatic, but still seemed more a skit than a feature-length film. "You could do maybe a good half hour of this thing," he thought. Then, a couple of nights later, he had yet another dream, this time set in a black neighborhood. "I said to myself, 'Oh, this is Harlem, I recognize the buildings.' I was watching this black man walk down the street. He was obviously a little bit frightened and he looked really lost. Then I realized—the way you realize things in dreams without seeing anything dramatized, or anybody saying anything—

that, 'Oh, he's from another planet. No wonder he feels lost. He can't talk. How alienating, literally, that must be. How lonely he must be.'

"I woke up and I said, 'Yeah! I had this wild dream and, you know, that really could turn into something. What an interesting guide into a neighborhood, into a life a lot of people have never been able, or wouldn't be able, to go to.' "

Sayles combined the three dreams into *The Brother from Another Planet*—the story of a black alien whose ship crashes in Harlem, leaving him to wander around much like the fugitive yeti with the combination of sci-fi and comedy suggested by *Assholes from Outer Space*.[14]

FILMS ALTER DREAMS

Other filmmakers have developed the capacity for lucid dreaming. One who makes frequent use of this is screenwriter/director Paul Schrader. "I dream movies," says Schrader. "Literally I often have dreams of sustained narrative over a period of hours. I know this because I'll wake up, look at the clock, return to the dream. These dreams have characters, dialogue, plot development. I am also aware of the dreaming process; that is, I'll critique the 'dream story' as it occurs. I'll think, 'This is not a good scene,' 'I should drop this character,' or 'I need some action'—back up and 'redream' the scene."[15]

When I did a formal research study of how truly lucid (in the original sense of logically clear) "lucid dreams" are, I found that some contained major illogic about points that should automatically follow from knowing one is dreaming. For instance, lucid dreamers might still think that they could be physically harmed by a dream peril, that other characters would awaken remembering the same dream, or that they could write down events as they occurred and retain the account upon awakening. I found another subgroup of dreams that were not lucid in the sense that the dreams identified the fact that "I'm dreaming," yet were accurate in realizing they could fly and ignore other usual laws of physics, or that characters were not real people, but could be summoned and dismissed at will. Some explanations for these dreamlike abilities involved magic, but the most common one went, "I knew it wasn't real life, I thought it was a movie," or "I knew I was the director."[16]

While dreams shape film, director Jose Luis Boreau makes the point that viewing this modern medium has also changed how we dream: "Our dreams have been enriched by the movies. We witness events that would be difficult to live out in daily life (an incursion into the ocean floor) or which are patently unreal (the rebellion of an entire galaxy against the central power). Such indirect experiences, which were once impossible, now offer the subconscious suitable vehicles for expressing our eternal yearnings and preoccupations. On the purely formal level, they provide new ways of visualizing in our dreams—camera angles, slow-motion shots, combinations of colors and of black and white—techniques we have learned only in movie theaters."[17]

While writing this chapter, I had a dream that illustrated Boreau's point. I dreamed I was floating or gliding slowly over the ocean—deep, clear waters like those of the Caribbean. The low angle of the sun allowed two perspectives. One was of faint reflections on the surface of the water from sky, clouds, and shadows. But at the same time, I could look into the depths and make out dark shapes of coral reefs and shadowy hints of exotic fish swimming beneath the surface. I felt a glorious sense of promise as I gazed down into the water.

I recognized in that dream the memory traces of Stephen King's description from *Writers Dreaming* (quoted in the next chapter) of dreaming as analogous to diving in the ocean: the deeper one goes, the more bizarre the creatures become, but the harder they are to bring up intact. It also echoes the idea, repeated throughout this book, that the most useful dreams combine our waking reasoning (reflections on the surface) with their fantastic imagery (the exotic ocean fish). But the specific form of the dream—gliding low over tropical water—is not something I've experienced in snorkeling coral reefs or even while landing at coastal airports. Rather, it is the typical opening shot of any number of movies set at the seashore—and of Jacques Cousteau documentaries—making its way into my possible experiences directly from my history as a filmgoer.

DREAM DRAMA

Before turning, in the next chapter, to literature relying solely on the written word, there is the medium of drama—somewhere between film and novel. Theater was, of course, a precursor to film, but one with more emphasis on narrative and less on visual intensity. Dreams have made major contributions to drama also. Carl Jung used the play as a metaphor to explain the function of dreaming: "A dream is a theater in which the dreamer is himself, the scene, the player, the prompter, the author, the producer, the public, and the critic."[18]

In 1937, as a high school student, Ingmar Bergman had what he later called "the fundamental dramatic experience of my life." This was attending a performance of August Strindberg's 1901 work, *A Dream Play*.[19]

In this play, based more on the tone and form of his own dreams than on the content of a specific one, Strindberg strove to "imitate the inconsequent yet transparently logical shape of a dream." He wrote in the play's preface, "Everything can happen, everything is possible and probable. Time and place do not exist; on an insignificant basis of reality, the imagination spins, weaving new patterns; a mixture of memories, experiences, free fancies, incongruities and improvisations. The characters split, double, multiply, evaporate, condense, disperse, assemble. But one consciousness rules over them all, that of the dreamer; for him there are no secrets, no scruples, no laws. He neither acquits nor condemns, but merely relates; and, just as a dream is more often painful than happy, so an undertone of melancholy and of pity for all mortal beings accompanies this flickering tale."[20]

Strindberg is correct about the preponderance of unpleasant dreams; modern content analysis finds negative emotions in dreams outnumbering happy ones. It is remarkable, however, that he is one of few artists to notice this fact, even though it was theoretically available to all. Most writers still cling to the image of dreams as delightful flights from reality; witness all our metaphoric uses of "dreaming" to denote a wishful, happy fantasy. Strindberg carefully observed the actual characteristics of dreams, and incorporated them meticulously into his play. *A Dream Play* had a major impact on theater; through Strindberg, the Committee of Sleep instigated a modernist movement away from literalism.

Jean Cocteau, quoted at the opening of this chapter, wrote a play that flowed even more directly from a dream. One night, in his dream, he "witnessed, as from a seat in the theater, three acts which brought to life an epoch and characters about which I had no documentary information." This he transcribed as *Knights of the Round Table.*[21]

In 1919, William Archer was America's leading theater critic but aspired to be a playwright. His muse arrived in a dream of being kidnapped. Archer and his friends were held prisoner by "cultured barbarians applying a sort of torture by courtesy to Europeans ... The leading spirit on the barbarian side was a woman, whom I conceived as a singularly able personality." She became the title character of *The Green Goddess,* which was the smash success of the next theater season.[22]

In 1923, before he'd written most of his greatest poetry, William Butler Yeats won the Nobel Prize for Literature on the strength of his dramatic work. One of these plays was *Cathleen ni Houlihan* (1902), which he told his Dublin producers had come to him in a dream. The title is a traditional metaphor for Ireland, implying a *femme fatale* who requires young men to sacrifice themselves for her. Yeats's fanciful rendition of this old tradition helped to revive Irish nationalism.

The English dramatist Herbert de Hamel received the most remarkable help that the Committee has ever given any playwright: historic stories that translated directly into his acclaimed plays. "In recent years there has been a recurring dream wherein I open a large history-book, with covers made of olive-wood," Hamel reported. "It opens always at the beginning of some chapter. The author's perfection of style is a sheer joy, and each chapter not merely throws a new light on the customs and habits of the period, but is obviously working up to some amazing climax. The print is large and clear.

"As I read, the book speaks the lines out loud. There is only one condition imposed upon me. I must, in reading, keep up word for word with the voice of the book. If I drop behind, the covers close together and the voice ceases. It speaks very clearly and not too fast."[23] Hamel usually stumbled only when he came upon archaic words—old Cornish and such, which the book reproduced better than his conscious memory—although he'd studied history at Cambridge before devoting himself to the theater.

Although Hamel's experience of reading in dreams is unusual among the filmmakers and dramatists of this chapter—and indeed in the general population of dreamers—we will hear more such stories from the writers in the next chapter, whose dream life often borrows from their waking fluency.

3

THE STATELY PLEASURE DOME:

DREAM LITERATURE

On a summer night in 1816, the houseguests at Lord Byron's Swiss villa included nineteen-year-old Mary Wollstonecraft; her fiancé, Percy Bysshe Shelley; Claire Clairemont, who was both Mary's stepsister and Byron's mistress; and physician John Polidori. The group spent the evening telling ghost stories over the din of a raging thunderstorm. At bedtime, Byron challenged his guests to write their own horror stories. Several of the resulting tales were published, even Dr. Polidori's first literary effort, "The Vampyre," which served as a precursor to Bram Stoker's *Dracula*. But by far the most successful was Mary Wollstonecraft Shelley's. The night of the challenge, she had this dream:

> I saw the pale student of unhallowed arts kneeling beside the thing he had put together—I saw the hideous phantasm of a man stretched out, and then on the working of some powerful engine, show signs of life, and stir with an uneasy, half vital motion. Frightful must it be to mock the stupendous mechanism of the Creator of the world. He would hope that, left to itself, the slight spark

of life which he had communicated would fade. He sleeps but he is awakened; he opens his eyes, behold, the horrid thing stands at his bedside, opening his curtain and looking on him with yellow, watery, but speculative eyes.

Swift as light and cheering was the idea that broke in upon me. "I have found it! What terrified me will terrify others, and I need only describe the specter which had haunted my midnight pillow." On the morrow I announced I had thought of the story.[1]

The dream, of course, became what is arguably the classic horror story of all time, *Frankenstein.* The teenage author was pregnant by Shelley at the time of the dream, so the creation of a wondrous, monstrous entity undoubtedly had immense unconscious significance. However, the Committee of Sleep combined her personal issue with Byron's casual challenge into a creation that transcended both.

Man has consulted his nocturnal muse for as long as he has sought tales to entertain his peers. In the fifth century c.e., Synesius of Cyrene observed, "How often dreams have come to my assistance in the composition of my writings! They aided me to put my ideas in order and my style in harmony with my ideas; they have made me expunge certain expressions, and choose others. When I allowed myself to use images and pompous expressions, in imitation of the new Attic style [a "modern" fad that had disappeared by the sixth century c.e.] . . . a god warned me in my sleep, censuring my writings, and making the affected phrases to disappear, brought me back to a natural style."[2]

The Romantic writers were especially reliant on dreams. Mary's husband, Percy Bysshe Shelley, published a collection of his nocturnal experiences in *The Catalogue of Phenomenon of Dreams, as Connecting Sleeping and Waking.* Cristina Rossetti, whose painter husband's dream imagery was discussed in the first chapter, used hers in her poetry. An example is "The Crocodiles," which describes a fanciful version of the animal, encrusted with gold and polished stones. Her contemporary, Anna Kingsford, published an entire book of stories and poems based on dreams.

Carl Jung wrote that virtually all cultures have a concept of "small" dreams, which possess only mundane personal significance, versus "big" dreams, which have major societal or philosophical meaning. It was the "big" dreams, he said, that led to creative works—which often depicted just the image that Jung said gave such dreams their archetypal quality. Edgar Allan Poe's favorite of his own stories was "Lady Ligea," which was based on a dream of the title character gazing at him with compelling, luminous, "gazelle-like" eyes.[3] That may be why so many of the examples in this chapter are nightmares; they are well represented among the dreams that stay with us for weeks—and often for life.

Although many such dream stories are quite realistic, a high proportion of them reflect their origin by the surreal nature of their content. William Butler Yeats—who, as described in the preceding chapter, won a Nobel Prize for plays based partially on dreams—also utilized them in the poetry of his later years. "The Cap and Bell," whose story Yeats says he dreamed "exactly as I have written it," tells of a jester in a garden who "bade his soul rise upward / and stand on the window sill."[4]

Another writer of the same period, Katherine Mansfield, turned an unusual dream experience into the successful short story "Sun and Moon." It is an impressionistic tale seen through the eyes of a five-year-old boy. "I dreamed it all," Mansfield said.

"I didn't dream that I read it. No, I was part of it, and it played round invisible me. . . . In my dream I saw a supper table with the eyes of five. It was awfully queer—especially a plate of half-melted ice-cream." Mansfield was able to capture this childhood perspective in her story more fully than she could have imagined it awake.[5]

Charlotte Brontë intentionally incubated exotic dream experiences for use in her writing, with a technique similar to those of the visual artists described in Chapter 1. When she wished to describe something she had not experienced in waking life, Brontë would tell herself at bedtime to dream of it that night— and indeed she would. She attributes her passages about opium to this technique, insisting—unlike so many of her peers—that she had never actually indulged in the drug.[6]

Sir Walter Scott also purposely cultivated help from the Committee of Sleep, but in his case it seemed to be the hypnagogic state on the verge of waking that was most productive. It "was always when I first opened my eyes that the desired ideas thronged upon me . . . ," he reported. "This is so much the case that I am in the habit of relying upon it, and saying to myself, when I am at a loss, 'never mind, we shall have it at seven o'clock tomorrow morning.' " *Bride of Lammermoor,* which biographer John Gibson Lockhart called "the most pure and powerful of all the tragedies that Scott ever penned," was dictated in its entirety from bed directly upon awakening.[7]

The literature of philosophy also owes a debt to dreams, specifically three that René Descartes had on the night of November 10, 1619. Descartes did not record the dreams verbatim, but biographers who interview him did. The key element in the first dream was a great wind blowing Descartes against a church; he awakened in pain. The second dream was of a huge flash like lightning in his room, with electrical sparks lingering in the air, and the third was of opening a book to the passage: *"quod vitae sectabor iter?"* (What path shall I follow in life?) At this point, Descartes became lucid and decided to interpret the dream, arriving at the conclusion that it was telling him the path to truth lay, not in the beliefs of organized religion, but in the glories of science. All of his writings followed from this premise. Hence "Rationalism" arose from the most intuitive of all sources—the Committee.[8]

RECENT CONTRIBUTIONS OF THE COMMITTEE

Modern authors also continue to consult the committee. Graham Greene reported that "when an obstacle seems insurmountable, I read the day's work before sleep and leave the (unconscious) to labor in my place. When I wake, the obstacle has nearly always been removed: the solution is there and obvious—perhaps it came in a dream which I have forgotten."[9] In some cases, Greene was clear that the Committee was working through a dream. In a period of financial stress, he dreamed that he had been sentenced to prison for five years and separated from his wife. This dream served a dual purpose for his next novel, *It's a Battlefield,* both by providing him with impetus to get started on it and by giving him the basics of the plot. Another of his novels, *The Honorary Consul,* also began with a dream.

"Sometimes identification with a character goes so far that one may dream his dream and not one's own," Greene reports. "That happened to me when I was writing *A Burnt-Out Case.* The symbols, the memories, the associations of that dream belonged so clearly to my character Querry that next morning I could put the dream without change into the novel, where it bridged a gap in the narrative which for days I had been unable to cross." Greene recorded his dreams and allowed them to be published posthumously as *A World of My Own: A Dream Diary.*

C. K. Stead had decided that his novel *Until the End of the Century at the End of the World* should have a character's dream in every chapter, but trying to invent them yielded unconvincing products. He modified dreams of his own to better effect but was stuck without one that would suit the last chapter. Then he read Greene's passage quoted above and it inspired his own Committee—Stead also had a dramatic detailed dream in which he was his character dreaming. He awoke and immediately wrote it into the last chapter.[10]

The American writer William Burroughs noted, "A good part of my material comes from dreams. A lot of it is just straight transcription of dreams with some amplification, of course."[11] Jack Kerouac also used his dreams extensively in his fiction, and, like Greene, published his dream journal. His 1961 *Book of Dreams*[12] contains 250 reports. Its preface includes a key describing which characters in the dreams had appeared with different names in his novels *On the Road* and *The Dharma Bums.*

Eudora Welty had a series of dreams about bandits and a fair maiden at Natchez Landing. She transcribed these scenes just as they occurred and wove them into her story "The Robber Bridegroom." Welty's agent, Diarmuid Russell, himself a writer, published an article titled "An Experiment with the Imagination" in *Harper's* magazine the following year. He reported a series of his own dreams in which what he called "the interior intelligence" (a concept similar to the Committee of Sleep) supplied his dreamscape with characters and incidents that his waking imagination could not have invented. Building on these dreams and Welty's, Russell concludes, "These experiences have made me believe that if a man is willing to bend his will toward the effort of awakening his interior genius, he may succeed surprisingly and be delighted with swift visions."[13]

And with the whimsical quality of many dreams, it's not surprising that children's literature has benefited also. In explaining why the hero of his whimsical children's book, *Stuart Little,* is a mouse, author E. B. White wrote to his agent, "I will have to break down and confess to you that Stuart Little appeared to me in a dream, all complete, with his hat, his cane, and his brisk manner. Since he was the only fictional figure ever to honor and disturb my sleep, I was deeply touched, and felt that I was not free to change him into a grasshopper or a wallaby."[14]

NIGHTMARE NOVELS

Stephen King uses yet another metaphor for the Committee. When Naomi Epel interviewed him for her book *Writers Dreaming,* he told her, "I've always used dreams the way you'd use mirrors to look at something you couldn't see head-on," he says, "the way that you use a mirror to look at your hair in the back. To me that's what dreams are supposed to do. I think that dreams are a way that people's minds illustrate the nature of their problems. Or maybe even illustrate the answers to their problems in symbolic language.

"I guess probably the most striking example of using a dream in my fiction was connected to the writing of *Salem's Lot,*" King told Epel.

It was a dream where I came up a hill and there was a gallows on top of this hill with birds all flying around it. There was a hanged man there. He had died, not by having his neck broken, but by strangulation. I could tell because his face was all puffy and purple. And as I came close to him, he opened his eyes, reached his hands out and grabbed me. I woke up in my bed, sitting bolt upright, screaming. I was hot and cold at the same time and covered with goosebumps. And not only was I unable to go back to sleep for hours after that, but I was really afraid to turn out the light for weeks. I can still see it as clearly now as when it happened.

Years later I began to work on *Salem's Lot*. . . . [As] I was looking around for a spooky house, a guy who works in the creative department of my brain said, "Well, what about that nightmare when you were eight or nine years old? Will that work?" And I remembered the nightmare and I thought, "Yes, it's perfect."

I turned the dead man into a guy named Hubie Marston who owned a bad house and pretty much repeated the story of the dream in terms of the way he died.[15]

At times, his dreams supply King with very specific solutions to current dilemmas, as when he was stuck on his book *It:*

When I'm working, I never know what the end is going to be or how things are going to come out. I've got an idea what direction I want the story to go in or hope it will go in, but mostly I feel like the tail on a kite. . . . And if I know when I sit down what's happening or what's going to happen, that day and the next day and the day after, I'm happy. But with *It,* I got to a point where I couldn't see ahead any more. And every day I got closer to the place where this young girl . . . they were going to find her.

I didn't know what was going to happen to her. That made me extremely nervous. Because that's the way books don't get done. All at once you just get to a point where there is no more. It's like pulling a little string out of a hole and all at once it's broken and you don't get whatever prize there was on the end of it.

So I had seven, eight hundred pages and I just couldn't stand it. I remember going to bed one night saying, "I've got to have an idea. I've got to have an idea!" I fell asleep and dreamed that I was in a junkyard, which was where this part of the story was set.

Apparently, I was the girl. There was no girl in the dream. There was just me. And there were all these discarded refrigerators in this dump. I opened one of them and there were these things inside, hanging from the various rusty shelves. They looked like macaroni shells and they were all just sort of trembling in a breeze. Then one of them opened up these wings, flew out and landed on the back of my hand. There was a sensation of warmth, almost like when you get a shot of Novocain or something, and this thing started to turn from white to red. I realized it had anesthetized my hand and it was sucking my blood out. Then they all started to fly out of this refrigerator and to land on me. They were these leeches that looked like macaroni shells. And they were swelling up.

I woke up and I was very frightened. But I was also very happy. Because then I knew what was going to happen. I just took the dream as it was and put it in the book. Dropped it in. I didn't change anything. . . . I really think what happened with this dream was that I went to sleep and the subconscious went right on working and finally sent up this dream the way that you would send somebody an interoffice message in a pneumatic tube.

King also describes these unconscious messages with the most time-honored metaphor: that of the ocean and its depths.

I think that our minds are the same nutrient bath all the way down to the bottom and different things live at different levels. Some of them are a little bit harder to see because we don't get down that deep. But whatever's going on in our daily lives, our daily thoughts, the things that the surface of our minds are concerned with eddy down—trickle down—and then they have some sort of an influence down there. And these messages that we get a lot of times are nothing more than symbolic reworkings of the things that we're concerned with.

King emphasizes that it is in the most shallow sleep that logical ideas arrive. He continues the metaphor by observing that we are used to seeing fish near the surface. The deeper ones are more exotic—translucent, fluorescent, trailing strange frills. These are wondrous in their own habitat, he says, but usually turn into "exploded fish, a total mess" if we attempt to bring them up to the waking world.[16]

Another of America's leading names in horror, Anne Rice, also told Epel she uses dreams—both fortuitous ones and those more intentionally provided for her books:

> Two dreams I've recently had definitely worked their way into my writing. They are dreams of flying and they have been absolutely wonderful. The feeling of rising up out of my body, free of it and just taking off. Those two dreams have been incredible and I know that they were inspired by the writing . . . the vampire in my later books can fly . . . I've had flying dreams for years . . . I just remember going up out of my body, that wonderful feeling. There's nothing like it that I've ever felt—to rise up like that in the dream. It's so vivid. The last time I had a flying dream I knew I was really doing it. I was aware but I was also really there. It was fabulously real.

In another dream, Rice was performing a ritual to call down the rain and reached up her hands until snow actually fell. She put this scene into another novel.

Like Graham Greene, Rice reports that she has dreamt her characters' dreams. "In a recent dream I had that struck me with that otherworldly quality, I was one of my characters. I was the vampire Lestat, my hero. I was trying to go up the side of a castle. I threw a star-shaped thing way, way up in the air so that it held fast to the edge of the battlements. Then I climbed the rope that was attached to it. That was a very, very shockingly vivid dream. . . ." She used this to elaborate the vampire's movement in a later book.

"Dreams have not so much changed my work as deepened it,"

Rice observes. "Take the flying, as an example. Before the dream I didn't get the real way it felt, how really great it felt; that incredible shooting up to the ceiling like a bubble being released, then straightening out beneath the ceiling and having no weight and moving out. That's really a deepening of the sensuous aspects of flying. And I can take that back to the typewriter or the computer and try to get that down."[17]

LITERARY FICTION

William Styron told Epel that he too owes his best-known work to the Committee of Sleep:

> I think it was 1974. I'd been working on a book that was not coming together for me at all. I had been slaving away at it and was getting very upset over the fact that it wasn't proceeding well. And one morning I woke up with this lingering vision. I don't like to characterize it as a dream, although I think it had the aspects of the remnant of a dream. I think there was merging from the dream to a conscious vision and memory of this girl named Sophie. . . . And it was powerful because I lay there in bed with the abrupt knowledge that I was going to deal with this as a work of fiction. That I had to abandon the other book I was trying to do and, because of her, because of all the resonance surrounding her story, I was suddenly going to have to write the book which later became *Sophie's Choice*. That very morning, I remember I walked over to my studio and wrote down the first words

just as they are in the book, and went from there to the end without any deviation to speak of. So in a sense, you could say that the whole concept of the book was, if not the product of a dream itself, the product of some resonance that a dream had given me.[18]

D. M. Thomas had a vivid dream that became first a short poem, then a longer one, and eventually his best-selling novel, *The White Hotel.* The first poem, "House of Dreams," read in part:

> It is a honeymoon hotel
> visited by the dead and the living.
> They share the same taxis, and a fool
> has muddled all the reservations. . . .
> Sappho is there, and Jung, and Freud,
> and the girl you shared a train journey with. . . .[19]

"I already had the idea I wanted to write a novel in the style of Freud's case studies," Thomas told me when I interviewed him at his cottage in Cornwall. "I was searching for the story. Other elements were circling in my imagination. My mother had died recently. The dream brought all the elements together. It was like an embryo to the novel: Freud was there, death was there, the train was there. I can still see myself riding in the black taxi and arriving at the hotel—that was the most memorable part of the dream."

Thomas wrote another poem titled simply "The Dream,"[20] which captured an interaction with his deceased father "as exactly as I could get it into words."

Doris Lessing had a series of dreams about a king and a seal in a cold oceanside setting that evolved like a story over several years. She made them into the novel *The Summer Before the Dark*. However, she waited for the last dream to present a conclusion, and the Committee deserted her—there was no final dream. She eventually decided she could complete it on her own and devised a happy ending she felt fit the progression of the dreams.[21]

In an opposite scenario, Isabel Allende wrote most of her first novel, *House of the Spirits,* without help from the Committee until she was stuck on the epilogue. "I knew how the book would end, I knew what I wanted to say and I knew why I had written it. Still, I had written the last fifteen pages more than ten times and I could never get it right. It was solemn, preachy—too political, melodramatic. I couldn't get the tone. One night, at three o'clock in the morning, I woke up with a dream."[22]

In the dream Allende was with her grandfather (dead in waking life). She sat by his bed where he lay dressed in black. Attired in mourning garb, she sat patiently recounting the entire plot of her novel to him. When she awoke, she realized that in writing the book, she had been telling the story to her dead grandfather all along. The tone of the book was her voice to him. Immediately she knew the epilogue needed to be the protagonist's grandfather dying and her sitting by his bedside telling him a story while she waits for dawn to bury him.

Anne Rivers Siddon was similarly stuck with the ending of her novel *Peachtree Road.* "I was not sure what to do with the main character of Lucy Bondurant," Siddon says in an interview for *Writers Dreaming.* "She was a very troublesome, beautiful, and charismatic woman who had caused great pain and destruction for herself and other people. I felt that some resolution, some closure, was going to be necessary for Lucy at the end of the book but I didn't know what. I literally dreamed a scene from start to fin-

ish and woke up thinking, 'Of course, it just has to be that way.' "
Siddon shows the curious half-ownership that many writers feel
for the productions of their dreams when she reports that her first
thought was "Why didn't I think of that?" She speculates, "I
suppose I may have had it all along, but dreams are the channel
that bring the good part of us, the free part of us, out into the
open."[23]

NOCTURNAL REWRITES

Writers may not even know they are stuck on an ending before
the Committee takes the initiative to provide that "free part of
us." Indian novelist Bharati Mukherjee told Epel:

> In the stories I've ended up liking, and in the novel
> *Jasmine,* the endings have definitely come to me in
> dreams. The very first time it happened was in my second
> novel, *Wife.* The ending took me by surprise. *Wife* is
> about a young woman who comes as an immigrant wife
> to New York and has a great deal of difficulty adjusting
> to the new world. I thought that like a pliant, good, obe-
> dient Indian wife, she would probably either give in to
> her depressions or commit suicide, which is a traditional
> and honorable way out for women like her. But instead,
> in my dream, she decided to kill her husband. The first
> thing I said to my husband as he woke up was, "I got it!
> The guy's going to die!" Therefore I wrote the novel in
> which the wife, in a misguided but very self-assertive act
> that was very important to me personally, actually does

murder her husband while he's having his breakfast. And so the poor husband bleeds into his Wheaties."[24]

In her short story "Buried Lives," Mukherjee planned that her protagonist, an illegal alien, was going to drown as he was smuggled by boat into Nova Scotia. But then she dreamed that he found a girlfriend in Germany who was willing to marry him, and didn't get on the boat after all. All of Mukherjee's dreamed revisions have characters rebelling against the conventional course her waking mind has planned for them, which is obedient and often masochistic. In her novel *Jasmine,* the title character was again about to take the socially acceptable way out of a crisis when Mukherjee dreamed that she instead boldly picked up and headed for California. It is no surprise to those of us working with dreams for psychotherapy rather than artistic production that they are a good medium to cut through social conventions and see around our repetitive patterns of behavior.

Many of the dreams incorporated into fiction are easily interpretable as simple Freudian notions of wish fulfillment on the part of the dreamer. But this doesn't prevent them from producing works of art for others. Clive Barker's short story "Age of Desire" is about the first man to test a potent aphrodisiac. Instead of being eliminated from the body, the drug proved able to regenerate and intensify itself. Barker based the story on a vivid dream in which the world was becoming more and more incredibly sexualized.

John Nichols dreamed of wandering through a field of bodies that had been blown apart, trying to get them back together—searching for the right head for a particular body, attempting to put limbs in place—but to no avail. One could see this as a classic personal post-traumatic dream, but Nichols also used it to power-ful dramatic effect as the recurring nightmare of the main char-acter in his Vietnam War novel, *American Blood.*[25]

Another landscape of angst, *Angela's Ashes,* was reshaped by a dream. Author Frank McCourt struggled with how to tell his painful real-life story without sounding unremittingly grim. The idea of using a child narrator came to him in a dream. The inno-cent, even humorous voice lightened the tone of the book and played a large role in its enormous success.[26]

While her brother was missing in action during World War II, Barbara Cartland—later known for her romance novels—dreamed he appeared to her. He had bullet wounds in the spots where she later learned he'd been fatally wounded. Despite the sense that she was being informed of his death, the dream was happy in the way that many bereaved dreamers take joy in vivid imagery of reuniting with loved ones. So when Cartland wrote the dream as a poem she titled it, without irony, "Alive."[27]

THE COMMITTEE DICTATES DIRECTLY

So far, we've been discussing dreams that occur as images and narratives and are then described in words upon awakening. However, there are purer forms of "dreamed literature." Words are rare in most people's dreams—even spoken ones, much less written. The research article "We Do Not Dream of the Three R's"[28] reports that well under one percent of all dreams contain a written word, and a minority of people recall *ever* having had a dream containing written words. People who earn their living by the written word often seem to be an exception to this rule.

After Thackeray completed a novel and was searching for his title, he simply dreamed the two words that are now a household name: *Vanity Fair*. In Katherine Mansfield's dream, cited earlier, of being a boy of five, the only words that appeared were at the end. She was given the title: "Sun and Moon."[29]

Alan Gurganus—best known for his novel *Oldest Living Confederate Widow Tells All*—received both the plot and title of another story from the Committee. He dreamed of standing at the kitchen window of a suburban home and seeing a figure "the color of a caucasian" fall in his backyard with a "thunk." Just before he awakened, the words "It had wings" appeared, emblazoned over the library door. Gurganus gave the story that title and made the narrator a housewife who tries to minister to a fallen angel.[30]

Novelist and poet Maude Meagher experiences what she calls "word dreams." She reports, "I dream the words as printed on a page before me, and create them as I read. The text is never anything that I can remember having read."[31]

When Robert Nye was 13, he fell asleep at the seaside cottage his parents were renting. He dreamed the rain came down with a pattern that evolved into a rhythmic stream of words which made up a poem about the rain. When he awoke, Nye wrote it down verbatim, adding only punctuation and the title "Listeners." He recalls, "It seemed to me at that moment I had fallen awake. I knew what I had to do for the rest of my life." Nye's *Collected Poems* begins with "Listeners."[32]

The most famous and lengthy example—though not the most reliable—of dreaming verbatim wording is Samuel Taylor Coleridge's description of the origin of his poem "Kubla Khan," which begins,

In Xanadu did Kubla Khan
a stately pleasure dome decree,
where Alph the sacred river ran
through caverns measureless to man
down to a sunless sea.[33]

By Coleridge's account, he fell asleep and dreamed of both the images of the palace and the specific words describing it. He awoke and wrote down the fifty-four lines that now exist, but then was interrupted by a caller. Upon trying to resume his writing an hour later, all but a few other lines and images had disappeared forever. Biographers have made two amendments to this account. First, Coleridge was known to have a heavy opium habit at the time he wrote "Kubla Khan," so it is extremely likely the sleep was drug-induced, rather than entirely natural dreaming. Second, multiple drafts of the poem have been discovered, which belies Coleridge's account. Still, most historians believe the basic description of his dreaming it in some sort of sleep and recording much of it upon awakening is accurate.[34] Many years later, Coleridge also dreamed (without the aid of opium) an epitaph for himself in quatrain verse.

Voltaire dreamed one canto of *La Henriade*. He remarked that he knew other poets, scientists, and mathematicians who created wonderful things in their dreams. Unfortunately, he didn't describe these, and given his associations with most of the great minds of eighteenth-century Europe, many wondrous examples seem to have been lost to posterity.[35]

A. C. Benson said of his "Phoenix" that "I dreamed the whole poem in a dream, in 1884, I think, and wrote it down in the middle of the night on a scrap of paper by my bedside."[36]

Sometimes the Committee steps in at the stage of revision. When James Mackerath was composing "The Death of Cleopatra," there came a point when it was complete except for two passages that troubled him. The Committee apparently targeted these. Mackerath awoke and wrote some lines down in the middle of the night without lighting a candle and went immediately back to sleep. In the morning he struggled to read the crudely penciled words on crushed scraps of paper and envelopes and found them "sane, fitting, and not unbeautiful." He incorporated them verbatim into the places that awaited them with a change of only one word. Mackerath adds that in the earlier moments of the waking consciousness in the morning, he had no recollection of either the passages or the fact that he had recorded them.[37]

John Masefield's poem "The Woman Speaks" came to him in a dream of "a tall lady dressed for out-of-doors with furs and a picture hat." In the dream, he knew of her past, and that she was in Lincoln's Inn Fields on a Sunday morning. As she moved out of the dream "the whole of the poem appeared in high relief on an oblong metal plate," from which he simply copied it down.[38]

The phenomenon of dreamed poetry was reported so often that it became the target of one writer's sarcastic wit: "Historically, the model of dream creativity is the nineteenth-century Romantic poet. Bolting upright in his four-poster bed, full of sudden inspiration, the Romantic poet would scribble a dream verse on his nightgown. The nightgown is an indispensable part of the creative act; according to that irreverent historian A. J. Liebling, the decline of lyric poetry can be shown to coincide with the exit of the male nightgown."[39]

Occasionally the same phenomenon happened without a

recalled dream. Trying to write a ballad with the refrain "Only the song of a secret bird," the Pre-Raphaelite poet Algernon Swinburne found to his irritation that it would not come for him, and went disconsolately to bed. In the morning he was able to write it out without so much as a pause. In Swinburne's case, he was not aware of having dreamed. The first three stanzas of "A Vison of Spring in Winter," he noted, came in the course of a night when he was neither dreaming nor on the borderline of sleep, but in a sound slumber from which he awoke to write them down. The next morning he feared to find them nonsense, but they needed no alteration.[40]

Never Mind . . .

The Committee has been observed to veer far off course with a few of its productions. Edwin Carpenter tells how a poet, who kept a pencil and paper by his bedside for such occasions, once awakened "feeling himself drenched with a sense of seraphic joy and satisfaction, while at the same time a lovely stanza which he had just dreamed lingered in his mind." He quickly wrote it down and went immediately back to sleep. In the morning he remembered the experience and, turning to look at the words "which he doubted not would make his name immortal," he read:

> *Walker with one eye,*
> *Walker with two,*
> *Something to live for,*
> *And nothing to do.*[41]

In a similar anecdote, another poet awoke feeling he had dreamed a poem more sublime than anything he'd composed awake. But, he bemoaned to his wife, it had already vanished from memory forever. No, she told him—all was not entirely lost. He'd been murmuring in his sleep. "I did luckily hear the last lines," she reported, "and I am sure I remember them exactly; they were—

> " '*By Heaven, I'll wreak my woes*
> *Upon the cowslip and the pale primrose.*' "[42]

These comic examples highlight that which is true of much dreamed language—that vocabulary and grammar are well preserved, rhyming possibly enhanced, while logic and meaning suffer. The relative importance of these factors for different genres is probably why so much successful dream literature is poetry.

Sometimes even the illogic of dream-thinking combined with its sense for the sound of language can result in delightful puns. Kenneth Atchity, novelist and writer of books on writing, had a dream that found a place amid the whimsical prose of one of his published books. The whole of "The Tom Otto Plot" runs for several pages, but this short excerpt gives a sense of its tone:

> "Grape, grape, grape," the Senator nearly wined. He barked a command to the door. "Rosemary, cummin here." His voice was aspic.
>
> "Yes, Basil," said the secretary, briskly endiving through the entrance. She walked on the bulbs of her feet as if she had onions.
>
> "I'm guava to the mushroom for a potatoble with my consistency here. Contact me if an escarole call comes up."

"What about your meeting with the Lemon Aid Society?" she asped.

"Tell them to grow on without me," the Senator shuckholed. "I can always catsup when I get back from bunch."

Atchity remembers, "I woke up laughing and started scribbling furiously before the puns evaporated. I guessed at a few words when my recall failed . . . the actual dream was longer. . . . No one can believe it was a dream. I barely can—yet I dreamed it." The dialogue appeared in his *The Three Sisters.*[43]

While Freud described dreamed language (he meant mostly spoken) as "infantile," and Emil Kraepelin, the founder of modern psychiatric diagnosis, called it "pathological," the largest study to date, *Language and Its Disturbances in Dreams,*[44] confirms what Atchity's example suggests. Psycholinguist Frank Heynick found that dream speech (at least as recalled) is lexically, morphologically, and syntactically well formed. Although at times it is illogical in content, it can also be "linguistically creative."

But sometimes all—including logic—is preserved, as Robert Penn Warren has experienced. He says of the larger group, "I dream a lot of dreams and most of them are comic and I wake up laughing. . . . I dreamed a whole poem once, but I'm sure-to-God not proud of it. . . . I could tell you some (dreamed) jokes, though!"

However, occasionally Warren has had coherent dreams that have aided him greatly in the realistic novels he has published, such as *All the King's Men.* "I've dreamed many nights the next scene of a novel I've been working on, in great detail, even dialogue. One time just in a couple of dreams (which solved a novel) and in my last one, almost every night for months. It's nice to get to the typewriter with half your work done.[45]

A final note on dreams and language—the Committee has *invented* two written language systems. In 1879, the German linguist J. Schleyer had mastered more than fifty languages and was seeking to create an amalgam language to facilitate international communication. In a dream, the necessary letters, base words, and processes for expressing common patterns appeared to him "in an orderly array." Schleyer named his new language Volapuk. Although it never enjoyed more than minor use, it is treated as a serious contender by linguists cataloging the ultimately ill-fated history of the struggle for a universal language.[46] More significantly, a dream did dictate the written language of an entire nation. But we'll save that for Chapter 8's discussion of non-Western cultures.

STEVENSON'S BROWNIES

Robert Louis Stevenson wrote most extensively and articulately about how his passion for writing interacted with his remarkable dreams, which he described as occurring in "that small theater of the brain which we keep brightly lighted all night long." He personified the designers of these dramas as his "little people" and, from an early age, said their productions were so vivid and moving that his dreams were more entertaining to him personally than any literature.

When Stevenson was young, "the little people had not as yet received a very rigorous training; and played upon their stage like children, rather than like drilled actors." But as he began to train as a writer and sell his work, "The pleasure had become a business, and that not only for myself, but for the little people of my theater. They understood the change as well as I. When I lay down to prepare myself for sleep, I no longer sought amusement, but printable and profitable tales; and after I had dozed off in my box-seat, my little people continued their evolutions with the same mercantile designs. . . . Behold! [They] labored all night and set before me truncheons of tales upon their lighted theater. . . ."

He said of the little people, or "Brownies," "They share plainly in [my] training, they have learned like [me] to build the scene of a considerate story and to arrange emotions in progressive order, only I think they have more talent." He offered the example of their role in the creation of his *Dr. Jekyll and Mr. Hyde:* "I went about racking my brains for a plot of any sort. On the second night, I dreamed the scene at the window, and a scene afterward split in two in which Hyde, pursued for some crime, took the powder and underwent the change in the presence of his pursuers." Stevenson described watching "with growing exaltation at my own cleverness (for I take all the credit), and at last a jubilant leap to wakefulness, with the cry, 'I have it, that'll do!' "

Sometimes he observed (like the author of "Walker with one eye . . .") that "the little people had gone stumbling and maundering through their parts and the play, to the awakened mind, is a tissue of absurdities." Stevenson believed at these times he was "too deep asleep so that the little people are drowsy too." This was a poetic statement of what we now understand in more neurological terms. As we've seen, dreams do need arousal to have true narrative coherence, and dozing, hypnogogic dreams often do this best.

Stevenson goes on to speculate on the nature of the Committee: "Who are they then? My Brownies, who do one-half my work for me while I am fast asleep, and in all human likelihood, do the rest for me as well, when I am wide awake and fondly suppose I do it for myself. For myself—what I call I, my conscious ego, the denizen of the pineal gland unless he has changed residence since Descartes [ironically, DNA research pioneer Francis Crick has recently suggested that free will is located in a deep fold in the cerebral cortex called the anterior cingulate sulcus]—I am sometimes tempted to suppose he is no story-teller at all . . . so that, by that account, the whole of my published fiction should be the single-handed product of some Brownie, some Familiar, some unseen collaborator, whom I keep locked in a back garret, while I get all the praise and he but a share. . . . I am an excellent advisor, I pull back and cut down; and I dress the whole in the best words and sentences that I can find and make; I held the pen, too; and I do the sitting at the table which is the worst of it.[47]

In this quote we see many of the theses to be developed in this book: that dreams may provide quite intentional help, that the Committee may be at work at other times but gets its best hearing in the dream state, and that the most useful dreams are close to waking. But first we will see how the Committee works in people developing other talents. The overlap with waking goals that Stevenson observed becomes even more important when dreams need to incorporate music, math, or other modes equally foreign to our usual sleep.

4

THE DEVIL PLAYS THE VIOLIN:

DREAMS AND MUSIC

"**Y**esterday," by Paul McCartney, has been recorded by more than two thousand artists and played six million times on American radio—two million times more than any other song ever written.

The tune originated in May 1965. At twenty-two, McCartney was already wildly famous. The Beatles were in London filming *Help!,* and Paul was staying in a small attic room of his mother's house on Wimpole Street. One morning, in a dream, he heard a classical string ensemble playing:

"I woke up with a lovely tune in my head," he recalls. "I thought, That's great, I wonder what that is? There was an upright piano next to me, to the right of the bed by the window. I got out of bed, sat at the piano, found G, found F sharp minor 7th—and that leads you through then to B to E minor, and finally back to E. It all leads forward logically. I liked the melody a lot, but because I'd dreamed it, I couldn't believe I'd written it. I thought, 'No, I've never written anything like this before.' But I had the tune, which was the most magic thing.[1]

"First of all I checked the melody out, and people said to me,

'No, it's lovely, and I'm sure it's yours.' It took me a little while to allow myself to claim it, but then like a prospector, I finally staked my claim; stuck a little sign on it and said, 'Okay, it's mine!' It had no words. I used to call it 'Scrambled Eggs'. The lyrics used to go, 'Scrambled eggs, oh, my baby, how I love your legs. . . .' There was generally a laugh at that point; you didn't need to do any more lyrics."

In the weeks that followed, Paul composed verses obliquely referring to his father's death. The piece was so different from what the Beatles were performing at that time that his bandmates suggested Paul record it as a solo. He prevailed upon them to join him, and the whole later string sound of *Sgt. Pepper's Lonely Hearts Club Band* was born.

"I got made fun of because of it a bit," Paul recalls. "I remember George saying, 'Blimey, he's always talking about 'Yesterday'; you'd think he was Beethoven or somebody.' But it is the one, I reckon, that is the most complete thing I've ever written. . . . For something that just happened in a dream, even I have to acknowledge that it was a phenomenal stroke of luck."[2]

Most people rarely hear music in their dreams: in fact, they don't hear much of anything at all. Calvin Hall and Robert Van de Castle, examining five thousand dreams from one thousand college students, found that only 1.5 percent of accounts contained any reference to sounds.[3] Music dictated through dreams is probably even rarer than the written word, though dream researchers have never specifically studied this. Brain activity in dreaming likely reflects waking priorities. This is a tenet of theories as diverse as Darwinian survival models and post-Freudian takes on interpersonal dynamics. Most of our sensory cortex is devoted to visual processing, as opposed to that of whales or bats, whose sonar is more powerful than their eyes. Human auditory centers are larger than those for some of our other senses, such as smell—represented in fewer than one percent of dreams in Hall and Van de Castle's study—but most of that space is used for processing spoken language.

Just as with writing, however, people who spend their lives composing music do have more brain area devoted to it, and they often encounter music in their dreams. The amount of music we hear while dreaming varies with the amount of attention we give it. Architect Lucy Davis, whose dream houses we encountered in Chapter 1, previously composed music. When she was doing that in her waking hours, her dreams often presented musical compositions. "For me, dreaming has always been a problem-solving state," Davis told me, "devoted to whatever kind of problem I'm working on."

Composers have many visual as well as aural dreams, so they may also view scenes that they later express in a musical piece. Some dream of examining completed scores. There's an even wider range in how music arrives in dreams than for the other arts. The surprised McCartney joined a long tradition of musicians aided by the Committee of Sleep. In fact, George Harrison's joking comparison to Beethoven was fortuitous; McCartney and the great composer did have a point of shared experience.

En route to Vienna in 1821, Beethoven dozed in his carriage and had his own encounter with the oneiric muse. He dreamed he was on a different journey—one to the Middle East. As he wandered through desert scenery, he heard an exotic canon playing—not exactly Middle Eastern music, but it was nevertheless unusual and enticing. "Scarcely did I awake when away flew the canon," he lamented, "and I could not recall any part of it." On returning from Vienna the next day in the same carriage, the composer found himself in a reverie about the previous day's lost music. In this state, close to sleep, with all the situational cues at hand, he heard the same music again playing in his head. Still awake, this time he held on to the music "as fast as Menelaus did Proteus" and transcribed it exactly. He later made changes in only three places.[4]

Memory for Dreamed Music

Beethoven's loss and recovery of dreamed material echoes what we've discussed in the literature chapter. The need for repetition is more common in later chapters' areas such as the sciences, where dreamed material grows more complex. As with Coleridge's "Kubla Khan," there are stories of music heard in dreams and only partially recalled. Even when the resulting piece is judged the composer's masterwork, he feels it is but a pale shadow of the Committee's creation. Sir Arthur Sullivan, the musical half of Gilbert and Sullivan, named a ballad "The Lost Chord" because he heard it in a dream but could only remember a few notes upon waking.[5] French composer Vincent d'Indy often woke with a faint memory of a composition, which he had to focus on with desperation to get even a few measures down.

More bizarrely, Giuseppi Tartini dreamed the Devil came and sat on his bed. The composer handed him a violin to see what he could do. The Devil played a haunting melody of unearthly beauty. The instant he awoke, Tartini grabbed his violin and tried to reproduce it. All he could remember was the distinctive double-stop trill. Around that marvelous sound, he composed a piece he called *The Devil's Trill Sonata*.[6]

The song "Dreamland" was also named for a partially remembered composition of the Committee. Lewis Carroll wrote the lyrics after his friend, the Reverend C. E. Hutchinson, dreamed of hearing the piece performed in an otherworldly amphitheater, but, upon awakening, could recall only the melody.[7]

The most amusing variation on this waking loss of dreamed treasures is a pair of lucid dreams recounted to me by former musician Bill Barton.

> I was about twenty-one years old, performing with a band, St John's Wood. We did rock and roll, but I had always loved big band music, especially Count Basie. The first dream was a morning dream—the dream right before waking up. I heard the most fantastic big band chart—very sophisticated section work—the saxes would play as a unit, then the trumpets as a unit. Call-and-response work, just exquisite harmony. All the elements of classical jazz were there. I knew at the time it was absolutely original—I was listening to it being formed. I thought it would be so wonderful to write it down. I was in the presence of something that my intellect was creating, but I knew I didn't have the facility—chops—for arranging that it required. I would have to settle for listening to it a few times. When I woke up, I thought it was just such a wonderful experience that I wanted it to happen again. And it did!
>
> A week later, about one in the morning, I dreamed a pop song. The lyrics were there, the music was there. I was above the whole thing, listening and saying, "That's really good!" I remember knowing in the dream that I

could wake up and write it down—I did have the capacity for this one. I was writing popular music at the time. But an angel on my other shoulder said, "You're not going to, are you? You could, but you're not going to! You slug, you're just going to listen to it and keep dreaming." And that's what I did. Much later, when I finally did wake up, it was gone—in the sense of enough detail to write down. There was just the smell of gunpowder after the fireworks are over. This time, remembering the dream, I had a different sensation—chagrined and embarrassed.

This anecdote reminds us that the dream muse needn't be heeded. The Committee of Sleep has other agendas. This book focuses on objective creation, but subjective personal issues normally occupy much more of our attention in dreams. Barton eventually decided that music was not his life's work. He now runs a business that tapes landmark case summations for lawyers' continuing education. His dream "angel" may already have been hinting at an alternative career.

FREQUENT MUSICAL DREAMERS

Singer/songwriter Billy Joel gets nightly memos from the Committee of Sleep. "I always dream music," he reports. "I know all the music I've composed has come from a dream. 'River of Dreams' had lyrics that began, 'I go walking in my sleep in the middle of the night. . . . ' " Joel says that he tends to dream musical arrangements rather than lyrics. He describes hearing one oneiric piece as classic choir voices without words and, upon awakening, writing it as a rock instrumental.[8]

Joseph Shabalala, founder of Ladysmith Black Mambazo and composer of two tracks on Paul Simon's Grammy Award–winning album *Graceland,* also hears all his compositions in dreams. He reports he's dreamed music every night of his life, always sung by a choir of children. In the dreams, "There is a stage, but there are children not on stage. They are between the stage and the sky, floating and always singing. They are like my teachers who teach me exactly this sound."[9]

Through the early sixties, Shabalala sang with various South African groups. None of them wanted to record the distinctive, intricate melodies that filled his dreams. In 1964 he recruited family and friends to form Ladysmith Black Mambazo to perform the nocturnal creations. By 1979, Ladysmith had recorded twenty-five albums, many of which were million-sellers in Africa. They were barely known off the continent, however, until Paul Simon heard a bootleg tape and flew to Africa to meet Shabalala. Their recording sessions yielded two songs for *Graceland:* "Homeless" and "Diamonds on the Soles of Her Shoes."

Global acclaim allowed Ladysmith to travel and perform around the world. They have recorded with Stevie Wonder, Julia Fordham, the Wynans, and Dolly Parton. They've worked on five movie soundtracks, and one of Shabalala's songs was adapted into the play *The Song of Jacob Zulu,* which earned six Tony nominations. Ladysmith is known for television appearances on Sesame Street and in commercials for 7-Up, Lifesavers Candy, Heinz Soup, and IBM. For better or worse, the Committee of Sleep can be said to have provided the music for all of these endeavors.

Shabalala's dream children sing in Zulu or combine it with other languages. He'd always edited their tunes, making them simpler and writing new words—until one recent album, fittingly titled *Journey of Dreams.* Of this album Shabalala says, "I feel the dreams are now living inside the music as never before. For the first time I have made the music on the record exactly as my dreams would tell me."[10]

Some musicians have been able to use dreamed words more consistently than Shabalala. The Committee has eclectic taste, judging by whom it favors. Richard Wagner, who composed many of the world's greatest operas, was one of the few who wrote the words as well as the music. In 1863 he told a friend about *Tristan and Isolde,* which may be his most intricate and demanding opera: "For once you are going to hear a dream, I dreamed all this: never could my poor head have invented such a thing purposely."[11]

The Committee supplied quite different music to Reverend Horton Heat, former pool shark and alumnus of the Eastern Texas Juvenile Correction Facility. This vocalist/guitarist/songwriter is at the forefront of the recent punk revival of rockabilly music. "The Rev" told NPR that his cult hit "Show Business" had played in his dream and he'd leaped up and written it down just as he'd heard it.[12]

Comedian and songwriter Steve Allen regularly heard music and lyrics in his dreams. The most successful song of his career was "This Could Be the Start of Something Big." He wrote it for a 1954 television musical, "The Bachelor," and later used it as the opening theme on "The Tonight Show." Allen reports, "I wakened from my sleep having just dreamed the catchy melody and four or five lines of lyrics. . . . I went to the piano and played the tune. The basic idea of it was all there in my dream, and when I awoke, I just wrote it down and finished it off."[13] Another such special-delivery song he titled "I Had a Dream Last Night About My Old Piano."[14]

VISUAL INSPIRATION FOR MUSIC

Compositions may also grow out of visual dreams. Igor Stravinsky recalls, "The idea of *Rite of Spring* came to me while I was still composing *The Firebird*. I had dreamed a scene of a pagan ritual in which a sacrificial virgin danced herself to death." Stravinsky composed the music to represent what he had seen, and originally staged it as a ballet. He was pleased with the music, but the choreography didn't equal his dream. He worked closely with the great Nijinsky on its first performance, but when it premiered in 1913, Stravinsky was disappointed with the results. When he saw Diaghilev's acclaimed version a decade later, he pronounced it "too gymnastic" to represent his nocturnal ballet. The composer came to prefer the unembellished concert piece as a more metaphoric way of capturing the dream's unearthly beauty. In what he saw as the final insult, Disney's film *Fantasia* featured cartoon dinosaur evolution choreographed to *The Rite of Spring*. Stravinsky described this sequence—much beloved by audiences—as "unresisting imbecility."[15]

European composer Gyorgy Ligeti was haunted by a dream he'd had as a boy. "In my early childhood," he recalls, "I dreamed once that I could not find a way through to my little bed ... because the whole room was filled up by a fine-threaded but dense and extremely complicated web, like the secretion of silkworms. . . . Beside me there were other beings and objects hanging up in the vast network; moths and beetles of every kind, trying to reach the light around a few barely glimmering candles. . . . Each movement of the stranded creatures caused a trembling carried throughout the entire system. . . . Now and then these movements, acting on one another reciprocally, became so powerful that the net tore in various places and a few beetles unexpectedly were set free, only to be lost again soon in the heaving plaitwork, with a stifling buzz. These events, occurring suddenly here and there, gradually altered the structure of the web, which became ever more twisted. . . ."[16]

Decades later, Ligeti composed *Atmospheres,* based on that childhood dream, starting with a complex but orderly "web" of notes into which discordant chords are introduced and embedded, creating an increasingly "twisted" counterharmony. Casual listeners might not "see" moths caught in a web, but to Ligeti, the orchestral composition perfectly embodied his dream vision.

Innovative modern composer Shirish Korde also has visual dreams leading to many of his compositions, but he simultaneously hears the music they are illustrating. He told me about the dream that presented him with *The Tenderness of Cranes.* "I was hearing fragments of music and seeing birds fly. The speed with which the birds were flying kept changing, which determined the musical gesture—the content of the passage. I wrote it as quickly as anything I ever wrote, in a weekend—Zen, all one stroke and it was done." The solo flute piece won both the Ettleson Composition Prize and the National Flute Association award for new music.

Another of Korde's dreamed compositions, *Rasa,* is a chamber opera based on Bharati Mukherjee's novel *Jasmine.* When I interviewed Korde, he had not heard the story of Mukjerjee dreaming the book's ending, described in the preceding chapter. But he had his own nocturnal adventure with it shortly after accepting the project and searching for music that would express the story. "Often in dreams," Korde observed, "I'll hear a sound that defines a piece, or movement, a percussion hitting in just a certain way. The opening of *Rasa* has no pulse, the image emerges from nowhere and blossoms. It emerged in a dream that way. I saw the image as colors in music, and saw notes in color. I was both hearing the music and seeing the notes. One passage of *Rasa* was all in red, so I staged it with red light."

Korde showed me his original scores for these and other dreamed pieces. He'd written one score in colored inks to reproduce the hue of the notes corresponding to the timbre of the sounds. Another manuscript is engraved with the exotic symbols his dream used to denote rhythm and timing. The notes of *The Tenderness of Cranes* resemble a pattern of birds flying across the page, even while observing the conventional staff positions.

Synesthesia is the term used by neurologists to describe experiencing sensations across modalities: seeing tones, hearing textures, tasting colors. Psychedelic drugs such as LSD greatly enhance synesthesia, but the phenomenon also occurs naturally in some people. Some are troubled by extreme forms of it during their waking hours. Russian neurologist Alexander Luria wrote about one patient who had such a pervasive experience of synesthesia that he was plagued by trouble seeing around the clouds of color generated by noises or hearing over the din of a texture. Neurologists think synesthesia is caused when inhibitory mechanisms fail and excitation spreads from one cortical sensory center to a neighboring one. Mild levels of synesthesia feel pleasant and enriching. Creative artists of all disciplines seem to have more synesthetic experience, both in waking imagery and in dreams, than do other people. For musicians this is, as for Korde, most typically their well-developed musical processes spreading into visual sensations.

The long out-of-print *Book of True Dreams* (Monteith, 1929) recounted an example of synesthesia similar to Korde's in a dreamed composition:

> I have in my possession a charming account of the experience of a lady belonging to our grandmother's day, who dreamed that she was listening to beautiful music. Guided by the sound, she entered a room where she beheld the musician, seated at an organ, playing from a manuscript. Looking over his shoulder, she saw that instead of the usual black heads and tails of the crotchets and quavers, the music was represented by a painting. The subject was a garland of flowers. On closer observation, she discovered that these flowers intertwined with horizontal lines, and then she saw that they were arranged in a certain order upon the lines and spaces of an ordinary stave, so forming a melody. When she awoke, the flowers, which in themselves made a melody of color, were forgotten; but she remembered their position as noted on a stave, and, with the music still in her ears, she was able to write down about three lines of manuscript, which has been preserved in the family (as a curiosity).[17]

Other Musical Gifts: Oneiric Instruments and Performances

Tuvan "throat singers" perform a type of vocal music native to the steppes of Asia—Tuva is a tiny country located in the exact geographic center of the continent. One group, Huun-Huur-Tu, has recently become popular in the West, touring as part of many ethnic music series. Tuvan men spend weeks alone with their horses on the vast plains, so many of the songs celebrate the bond between a man and his horse with a passion other cultures reserve for heterosexual love. When I saw Huun-Huur-Tu in concert, they began with "Lament of the *Igil,*" a traditional song inspired by a dream.

"Lament" recounts how the mare of a *noyon,* or feudal landowner, dies in labor. He orders her colt taken to the steppe and left there for the wolves so he won't have to pay for its food. Oskus-ool, the peasant who is told to abandon it, takes the colt home instead, and feeds it on goat's milk. The colt grows into a great gray stallion. Oskus-ool rides him in races and they begin to beat all the *noyon*'s horses. With each win, the horse and peasant become more famous throughout Tuva. The envious *noyon* orders his servants to kill the gray stallion by pushing him over a sheer cliff.

"Oskus-ool looked everywhere for his horse," the song continues, "and, unable to find it, fell asleep from exhaustion. Then, in a dream, he saw his horse speaking in a human voice: 'You'll find my remains under the sheer cliff. Hang my skull on an old larch tree, make a musical instrument from its wood, carve it with my image, cover it with skin from my face, and make the strings from the hair of my tail. When you start to play this instrument, my double will come down from the upper world.' "[18]

The peasant found his beloved horse's body and fashioned the instrument just as the horse had instructed in the dream. Then he began to play it, recalling how the colt and he had played together, how the stallion had won all the races. Oskus-ool flushed with anger as he remembered the treachery of the *noyon,* and all his grief and anger found their way into his music. Then, the song concludes, the clouds parted. Down from the highest mountain galloped an identical twin of the beautiful gray stallion.

Oskus-ool's dream had, of course, inspired the song. More remarkably, the design his dream called forth—the fiddle carved with a horse's head, covered with horse hide, and strung with horsehair—also came into being. The *igil,* or horse-head fiddle, is now the most popular accompaniment for Tuvan singers. As they perform "The Lament of the *Igil,*" they essentially reenact it. Tuvans say the *igil* is their most expressive instrument because Oskus-ool poured into it all his love, grief, and rage.

The tale of Oskus-ool's dream is no doubt distorted by its long oral tradition, but it is likely based on a real peasant's experience. A less poetic but better documented case of a musical instrument designed by the Committee of Sleep is that of Dr. Ernest Chladni. In 1789, Dr. Chladni was working on a glass musical instrument that would use to best advantage the sound properties of water-filled crystal glasses.

> On the second of June, being tired with walking, he sat down on a chair, about nine in the evening, to enjoy a short slumber; but scarcely had he closed his eyes, when the image of an instrument such as he wished for, seemed to present itself before him, and terrified him so much that he awoke as if he had been struck with an electric shock. He immediately started up in a burst of enthusi-

asm; and made a series of experiments which convinced him that what he had seen was perfectly right—that he now had it in his power to carry it into execution. He made his experiments and constructed his first instrument in so private a manner, that no person knew anything of it. On the eighth of March, 1790, his first instrument of this kind was completed, and in a few days he was able to play on it some easy pieces of music. To this instrument he gave the name of Euphon, which signifies an instrument which has a pleasant sound.[19]

Chladni's instrument enjoyed modest commercial success, but was upstaged by Benjamin Franklin's similar mechanized instrument, the glass harmonica. Chladni's invention is now relegated mostly to music history museums. It is also referred to as the "euphonium," but should not be confused with the equally obscure brass tubalike instrument of that name—an accomplishment of the waking intellect.

As well as helping design instruments, the Committee of Sleep also aids those performing upon them. Schonberg's biography of Vladimir Horowitz tells a story about the summer of 1951 when the great pianist rented a vacation house on Fire Island. This was also the summer residence of Leonid Hambro, then a staff pianist at WQXR, the classical music station of *The New York Times*. Horowitz's summer house was behind the tennis courts, and Hambro made a point of wandering there every day to eavesdrop on his practicing.

"One day," Hambro recalls, "I walked down the boardwalk, and there he was sitting and looking at the passersby." Hambro introduced himself. Horowitz got excited. "Your recording of Prokofiev's Sixth Sonata is the best I ever heard. In the last movement, that passage, how do you do the fingering?"

Hambro told Horowitz that he had literally dreamt that fingering. "Very frequently," he told Horowitz, "I dream fingerings. In my business I have to play about two hours of new music every week, so I try to find fingerings for accuracy."

Horowitz was enchanted. "That's very interesting," he said. "You know, I dream fingerings too. I thought I was the only one."[20]

Of course, no one is "the only one." In the chapters on science and inventions we will see that the Committee has designs far beyond musical instruments. In Chapter 7 we'll examine what it's taught the body to do in addition to piano fingerings. It is striking to watch people rediscover the creative power of dreams. Oblivious to history, they nevertheless repeat the patterns of visual representations combined with the artist's or inventor's predominant mode. The dream states closest to waking continue to be the most productive for most fields. Some creations go far beyond the usual capacities of their inventors. It's not surprising that our musicians chose to represent the Committee as the Devil in one example and an angel in another.

5

THE COMMITTEE OF SLEEP
WINS A NOBEL PRIZE: DREAMS
IN SCIENCE AND MATH

"**M**y mom first told me about menstruation when I was seven," biologist Margie Profet told me. "I thought it was the weirdest thing I'd ever heard of. When I was ten or eleven, the school gave information about reproduction to girls. They'd send the boys away. They had a film with cartoon drawings of a woman's body with ovaries and Fallopian tubes. In the cartoon, there was the uterine lining building up and the egg being released. Then it ended with this thing, like, if there's no pregnancy, it just gets rid of everything. A red flag went up and I thought, 'That doesn't make sense!' "[1]

Biology explained this major loss of blood, tissue, and nutrients as an inefficient part of the reproductive process. By the spring of 1988, Profet had become a biologist. She'd done work on pregnancy sickness and allergies, but had never considered studying menstruation when she had the following dream:

"In the dream I saw cartoon images of a woman's body, like the ones in the school film. The ovaries were pale yellow; the uterus was deep red. There were black triangles in the endometrium. Blood was coming out, taking the triangles with it. Then my cat meowed, wanting out—he was quite a nocturnal hunter. I woke up into this half-awake state and thought, 'The black things are pathogens—that's why!' I went back to sleep. The next morning I had this vague feeling, 'Did I have a dream last night?' I wandered around and then, 'Oh yeah!'

"That dream inspired the course of my research," Profet recalls. "I finished the allergy studies, of course, but then I spent three years studying menstruation."

Profet's dream-inspired theory posits that harmful bacteria enter the uterus and Fallopian tubes by hitchhiking on sperm. Menstruation eliminates the threatening intruders in two ways: the sloughed-off uterine lining carries microbes off, and the blood itself is rich in immune cells ready to engulf pathogens. Profet buttressed her theory with several electron-microscopy studies from the medical literature. One detected bacteria attached to the heads and tails of wriggling sperm. Others showed the rich supply of macrophage immune cells in menstrual blood—very much as in her dream.

Profet's theory and research earned her a MacArthur Foundation "genius" grant. Media outlets covered the story of her perceptive insight, and her work to prove it correct. "It's the only serious contender for a plausible evolutionary explanation of menstruation," says George Williams, an editor at the *Quarterly Review of Biology* "It is extremely unlikely that her theory is seriously wrong. Her arguments are quite convincing."[2]

Two network television shows featured animations of Profet's "Eureka!" experience. "It's so weird to watch your own dream on TV," she told me. "Neither of them ran the graphics by me. One had the colors wrong and the other had the triangles too big. I didn't know they were going to do it. I was just watching and all of a sudden, there was my dream. It happened *twice*."

Most creative dreamers are actively working on a given problem when their dreams step in with a suggested solution. Profet was not. "My other research was vaguely related. In pregnancy sickness, there's reproductive biology. In allergy, there's an acute response, vomiting, to expel something. But menstruation hadn't been a big deal to me since I first heard about it in school. Except maybe it sticks somewhere in my mind when something doesn't make sense," she reflects. "The one connection was that the day before, I was talking with one of my sisters about menstrual flow—just things like whether it was heavy or light."

After her major contributions to biology, this remarkable woman went on to do work at the intersection of physics and math. But she says, "Math and physics are not explicitly in my dreams. I'm intellectually happier than I've ever been; the last three years have been my most creative. But I'm not dreaming about my work, except for one dream that encapsulated it metaphorically—probably because it's more abstract."

Nor has Profet had any other problem-solving dreams. "I think of it as a once-in-a-lifetime thing," she says.

At the time of Profet's nocturnal cartoon, she'd heard of only one such "discovery" dream; "Now I've read about many others." The one she'd met in her scientific education was that of August Kekulé, a staple of many a lecture on organic chemistry.

"Let us learn to dream, gentlemen, then perhaps we shall find the truth," said Kekulé, while giving the keynote speech in 1890 to the German Chemical Society.[3] Kekulé's was not a once-in-a-lifetime experience—he recounted two such dreams in this talk. They were the foundations of his two main scientific achievements.

> During my stay in London I resided for a considerable time in Clapham Road. . . . I frequently, however, spent my evenings with my friend Hugo Muller at the opposite end of the metropolis. We talked of many things but most often of our beloved chemistry. One fine summer evening I was returning by the last bus, through the deserted streets of the city. I feel into a reverie [Traumerei] and lo, the atoms were gamboling before my eyes! . . . I saw how, frequently, two smaller atoms united to form a pair; how a larger one embraced the two smaller ones; how still larger ones kept hold of three or even four of the smaller; whilst the whole kept whirling in a giddy dance. I saw the larger ones formed a chain, dragging the smaller ones after them but only at the ends of the chain. I saw what our past master, Kopp, my highly honored teacher and friend, has depicted with such charm in his "Molecularwelt": but I saw it long before him. The cry of the conductor, "Clapham Road," awakened me from my dreaming; but I spent a part of the night in putting on paper at least sketches of these dream forms.

"This was the origin of the 'Structural Theory,' " Kekulé told his audience, referring to his now definitive explanation of how carbon bonds to other atoms. This provided the foundations for modern organic chemistry—an achievement so noteworthy it accounted for his former professor Kapp writing books about the twenty-five-year-old Kekulé's ideas.

Seven years later, Kekulé was struggling with the structure of benzene. Unlike every other compound, benzene's structure could not be described by the existing notational system. In his German Chemical Society speech, Kekulé recounted another dream that solved this problem:

> During my stay in Ghent, I resided in elegant bachelor quarters in the main thoroughfare. My study, however, faced a narrow side-alley and no daylight penetrated it.... I was sitting writing at my textbook but the work did not progress; my thoughts were elsewhere. I turned my chair to the fire and dozed. Again the atoms were gamboling before my eyes. This time the smaller groups kept modestly in the background. My mental eye, rendered more acute by repeated visions of the kind, could now distinguish larger structures of manifold conformation: of rows, sometimes more closely fitted together all twining and twisting in snake-like motion.
>
> But look! What was that? One of the snakes had seized hold of its own tail, and the form whirled mockingly before my eyes. As if by a flash of lightning I awoke; and this time also I spent the rest of the night in working out the consequences of the hypothesis.

The "consequence" was, of course that the benzene molecule was a ring, not a straight chain. Kekulé makes clear that he saw atoms on other occasions as well. It was always with his eyes closed and at least dozing. These visions seem to have occurred during the onset of hypnagogic sleep, not during the later deep sleep of REM periods. Kekulé had studied architecture in college, so it is not surprising that he took a highly visual approach to chemistry.

"Dreams and visions deserve to be recognized, without ridicule or pretense, as having an important place, even in modern chemistry," stated Eduard Faber at the 1996 Kekulé Centennial.[4]

THE ROLE OF THE HYPNAGOGIC STATE

Dreams solving scientific problems have much in common with the previous chapters' dreams on the arts—especially with the predominance of visual inspiration. Scientific dreams are more likely, however, to come from the hypnagogic state, which occurs immediately upon falling asleep or just before awakening. This is what Salvador Dalí's "Slumber with a Key" technique, described in Chapter 1, seeks to create. Both Profet's and Kekulé's dreams fall into this category. Dreams incubated this way provoke more logical thinking about what the visual images mean—which is consistent with what we know about hypnagogic states having a higher degree of activation. Hypnagogic dreams are the next closest state to waking in terms of brain-wave patterns. Previous chapters discussed how the "primary process" mode of thinking—visual, intuitive, emotional—contributes to creativity. For dreams promoting scientific discovery, the crucial factor may be that primary process, which characterizes dreams, coexists with "secondary process"—logical, linear, and focused—which usually dominates waking thought. In these hypnagogic, half-awake dreams, the two modes enjoy a rare interaction. The dreamer can critically evaluate images while they're still before the eyes.

Another point that deserves mention about dreams in science is that bogus anecdotes abound. The most popular is the myth that the structure of DNA was discovered in a dream. This fallacy seems to have grown from Kekulé's story. All versions of the alleged DNA dream likewise have snakes twisting around each other, sometimes grabbing one another's tails. Some accounts attribute the dream to James Watson, others to Francis Crick. One recent Web site perpetuating this story must have discovered it couldn't be traced specifically to either of the molecule's discoverers and therefore declared, "One night in 1953, as *one of the scientists* was sleeping, he had a dream. . . ." This despite the fact that Watson wrote a popular book about the discovery that makes it clear that it took place entirely in the waking world. After his work on the double helix, Crick went on to publish a theory of dreams in which he declared them to be meaningless information that the brain is discarding during REM sleep. What has flippantly been termed his "garbage disposal theory of dreaming" has been largely discredited—but that Crick proposed it renders ironic the allegation that he was ever a beneficiary of the Committee. In fact, the one time he was ever queried about dream creativity, Crick replied that "no one would deny that dreams may occasionally be amusing . . . but the evidence scarcely warrants the notion that dreams systematically convey useful information."[5]

Other myths have remarkable persistence. One purports that the structure of the atom was dreamed as an image of the solar system with the planets revolving around the sun. A peculiar detail of this account is that it attributes the discovery to the modern physicist Niels Bohr, when in fact it was described much earlier by Lord Rutherford. Much of this misinformation appeared for the first time in a 1961 book, *The Twilight Zone of Dreams.*[6] Stanford University sleep lab director William Dement has challenged many stories in the book, even personally writing to Niels Bohr. Much like Crick, Bohr replied that he'd "never had a useful dream," much less that particular one. Dement complains that the book apocryphally "credits dreaming with nearly every artistic and technical accomplishment by our race."[7]

These bogus anecdotes lead some scientists to dismiss altogether the idea of dream creativity. However, most of the classic stories do check out—even those that have been seriously challenged. In 1984 two science writers, J. Wotiz and S. Rudofsky, created a sensation in both dream research and chemistry by suggesting that Kekulé lied long after the fact about dreaming of the structure of the benzene molecule to conceal his reliance on earlier chemists' work. More-careful investigation, however, documented that Kekulé described a dream image from his first presentation of the paper and properly cited his predecessors. Much of Wotiz and Rudofsky's argument rested on what turned out to be faulty translations of German documents.[8]

Another spectacular success of the Committee occurred a few years before Kekulé's chemistry breakthroughs on the other side of the Atlantic. Louis Agassiz was the dominant figure in nineteenth-century American biology. One of the first academics of his stature to leave Europe for the New World, he contributed to many biological fields. A major work was his definitive compendium of all known fossil fish—identifying many of these himself. While he was working on this project, he was stumped for two weeks by a particular fossil. Extraction techniques at that time were less sophisticated than they are today; it was easy to ruin a fossil while trying to remove the surrounding rock if one did not already know its exact structure. The exposed portions of this fish were ambiguous, and Agassiz hesitated to classify it and begin extraction.

One night, at the height of his dilemma, Agassiz dreamed he saw the fish before him with all its outer features perfectly restored. When he awoke, he tried to fix the image in his mind, but it quickly faded. The next night he dreamed of his fish a second time, but as he awoke it disappeared as quickly as before. Not about to let this happen again, the third night Agassiz placed paper and pencil beside his bed. Toward dawn the dream fish reappeared. At first its image was vague, but gradually its structure grew distinct. In what he called "a still half-dreaming" state, Agassiz sketched the fish in total darkness and fell back asleep.

That morning he was surprised to see he'd drawn features quite different from any of his waking speculations. Hastening to his laboratory, he began to chisel away at the fossil in accord with the dream. The rock came away to reveal underportions of the fossil that matched his drawing perfectly. Once it was exposed, Agassiz easily classified the specimen.[9]

It seems to be the case that the more complex the field of endeavor, the more common is the phenomenon of repetition of a dreamed solution to a problem. Sometimes, in science, the task of the Committee seems to be to deliver a completed solution to consciousness rather than to solve it during the course of the dream. In the following example, it performed this task for an even more important discovery.

A Nobel Prize in Medicine

In 1936 the Nobel Prize in Medicine went to a contribution of the Committee of Sleep. Physiologist Otto Loewi had been studying how nerve impulses are transmitted within the body. The prevailing theory was that it was by direct electrical wave. This did not explain the fact that although electrical potential is constant throughout the body, stimulation of a nerve may increase activity in one organ while decreasing it in another. In 1903, Loewi learned that certain drugs mimic the inhibitory as well as augmentory electrical effects. He suspected that nerve terminals might contain chemicals similar to the drugs, which, when released, also stimulated or inhibited an organ. Loewi could think of no way to prove this theory, and he completely forgot it for seventeen years as he worked on other medical quandaries. Here is the 1920 inception of the prize-winning experiment, in Loewi's own words. Long after his death, it is impossible to know for sure whether he referred to a dream:

> The night before Easter Sunday of that year I awoke, turned on the light, and jotted down a few notes on a tiny slip of thin paper. Then I fell asleep again. It occurred to me at six o'clock in the morning that during the night I had written down something most important, but I was unable to decipher the scrawl. The next night, at three o'clock, the idea returned. It was the design of an experiment to determine whether or not the hypothesis of chemical transmission that I had uttered seventeen years ago was correct. I got up immediately, went to the laboratory, and performed a simple experiment on a frog's heart according to the nocturnal design . . . its results became the foundation of the theory of chemical transmission of the nervous impulse.[10]

In the experiment, Loewi electrically speeded up the beat of a frog heart. He then collected the liquid from around the pounding heart and poured it over another frog heart, which then also quickened its pace. *Voilà*—chemical transmission of the electrical impulse. He had performed a similar procedure two years before while testing a quite different theory, but his nighttime musing prompted him to try it with the frogs. "Most so-called 'intuitive' discoveries," Dr. Loewi offers, "are such associations made in the unconscious."

So the experiment that won the 1936 Nobel Prize in Physiology and Medicine was "made in the unconscious"—but was it *dreamed?* Some science historians believe Loewi's brainstorm occurred to him upon awakening. A few creative "Eureka!" solutions do happen this way. But when a breakthrough of this magnitude occurs in the waking state, it is unusual either to fall immediately back asleep or to have no memory of it the next morning. Loewi's amnesia when he couldn't read his writing is more typical of attempts to recall dreams. REM sleep and the brief awakening that may follow it are characterized by low levels of the chemicals that allow our brains to transfer short-term memories into long-term storage. Loewi's need to await a recurrence the following night is strikingly like Agassiz's recurring fish dream.

Even if Loewi's nocturnal experience was indeed a dream— and we cannot be certain it was—there would be no way of telling whether he dreamed of doing the experiment, of seeing its preparation set before him, or of a metaphoric inspiration for it. Many older biographical accounts of other scientific discoveries lack clarifying details even when they make it clear there was a dream. For example, at the turn of the century, Nevil Story Maskelyne dreamed the solution to a problem that had stalled the completion of his treatise on crystallography. His daughter reported just that he had been working hard on it, then had a "long dream" in a "deep sleep," and rose immediately to begin checking the accuracy of the dreamed answer.[11]

THE COMMITTEE CORRECTS "SOLUTIONS" OF THE WAKING WORLD

A scientific dream that was recorded with painstaking precision was that of the Assyriologist Herman Hilprecht. In early 1893, Hilprecht was writing a treatise on archaeological findings at the temple of Bel at Nippur. The original objects remained in Constantinople, so he was working from sketches made by the University of Pennsylvania's excavation team. Two fragments of agate from the ruins had eluded precise identification. Their discoverers presumed them to be pieces of ancient rings. One of the fragments contained the letters *KU,* so Hilprecht classified it as belonging to King Kurigalzu. He placed the other, similar piece on a page with unclassifiable fragments.

Once the final page proofs for his book were ready, he was still not satisfied with this solution. After poring over the proofs all evening, he went to bed about midnight. "Then," Hilprecht reported, "I dreamed the following remarkable dream."

> A tall, thin, priest of the old, pre-Christian Nippur, about forty years of age, and clad in a simple abba, led me to the treasure chamber of the temple, on its south-east side. He went with me into a small, low-ceilinged room, without windows, in which there was a large wooden chest, while scraps of agate and lapis-lazuli lay scattered on the floor. Here he addressed me as follows:

"King Kurigalzu [circa 1300 B.C.] once sent to the temple of Bel, among other articles of agate and lapis-lazuli, an inscribed votive cylinder of agate. Then we priests suddenly received the command to make for the statue of the god Ninib a pair of earrings of agate. We were in great dismay, since there was no agate as raw material at hand. In order to execute the command there was nothing for us to do but cut the votive cylinder into three parts, thus making three rings, each of which contained a portion of the original inscription. The first two rings served as ear-rings for the statue of the god; the two fragments which have given you so much trouble are portions of them. If you will put the two together you will have the confirmation of my words. But the third ring you have not yet found in the course of your excavations, and you never will find it." With these words, he vanished.

The next morning Hilprecht examined the sketches again. He was astonished to find that the two fragments indeed fit together to make a votive cylinder whose original inscription read, "To the god Ninib, son of Bel, his lord, Kurigalzu, pontifex of Bel, presented this."

Hilprecht changed his page proofs to reflect this discovery and sent the book to press. Other scholars accepted his interpretation until one Assyriologist pointed out that the sketches indicated the fragments were of different colors. This puzzled Hilprecht for months; he was sure the lettering could not be a coincidence. In August 1883 he was fortuitously invited to the Imperial Museum in Constantinople to assist their cataloging and study of the temple findings. Upon arrival, he described his dream and the quandary of the differing colors to the museum director, Halil Bey. The Middle Eastern scholar accorded more import to the dream than had Hilprecht's Western colleagues. Bey opened all the cataloging cases and encouraged him to make the fragments his first priority.

No one else had associated the two agate pieces, so Hilprecht found them in distant cases. One was predominantly gray, the other veined with white. However, it was quite obvious that the stonecutter's saw had divided one piece of rock along a natural vein in its coloration. "As soon as I found the fragments and put them together, the truth of the dream was demonstrated *ad oculos,*" wrote Hilprecht. Halil Bey, who had studied the larger details of the excavation, could also confirm another aspect of the dream—that the treasure chamber had stood at the southeast side of the temple. Hilprecht had found indirect clues to this, but had not held it as conscious knowledge before the dream.

Like Kekulé, Hilprecht had made a previous discovery through a dream. Ten years earlier his dissertation topic had been to translate the stone of Nebuchadnezzar. He had initially accepted the prevailing explanation of the ancient Assyrian's name as meaning "Nebu protect my mortar board"—i.e., protect my work as a builder. One night, after working late on other aspects of the stone's translation, Hilprecht had gone to bed around two. He woke from a dream convinced that the name should be "Nebu protect my boundary." After studying the Assyrian derivations, he decided that the end of the name, "nez-zar," was indeed closer to the word for *boundary* than to the one for *mortar.* He published the new translation, and it became universally accepted. Hilprecht could not recall this dream in the detail of his later one involving the priest of the Temple of Bel. He remembered only that it involved sitting at his work table and somehow arriving at the conclusion that awakened him.[12]

It is striking that both of Hilprecht's dreams involved corrections to existing "solutions" of scientific conundrums. His waking mind had arrived at solutions in both cases, but the Committee continued and dug deeper to find more accurate ones. British chemist Roman Kresinski had a similar experience recently with his research using X-ray diffraction to determine the crystalline structure of solid materials. He had puzzled over results that sometimes yielded a 2:1 analytical ratio when 3:1 would be expected. He nevertheless wrote up the paper based on the most obvious hypothesis, and published it as a preliminary finding.

The data for further stages of the experiment continued to puzzle him until one night Kresinski dreamed of another molecule—the one that a 2:1 ratio would predict. He suddenly realized he had identified the molecule incorrectly in his paper. "We have since verified these data and all are consistent with my dream," he told me. Although his group had to print a correction to the original paper, the "correction" proved more important that the original, and led to further publications.

Nevertheless, when Kresinski recounted his experience, he repeatedly described the dream as discovering that he'd failed to solve the original problem, rather than generating a helpful correction. "Perhaps it is after all a discovery rather than a disappointment," he said, "but I always associate it in my memory with a disappointment, because I was wrong in my *original* interpretation." Just as Paul McCartney didn't feel that he'd composed "Yesterday" because he'd heard it in a dream, Kresinski didn't allow himself full credit for his discovery.

COUNTING ON DREAMS

While anthropomorphized chemical molecules and cartoons about the workings of our body are hardly common in most people's dream landscape, mathematics is yet more foreign. The article cited in the literature chapter as arguing that writing is not a likely mode of dream expression views math as a complex anathema. Its title says it all: We Do Not Dream of the Three R's.

However, we do sometimes dream of math. In one of my own oddest dreams, my mother informed me that a dream character's appearance was determined by the position of the character in relation to the dreamer's sleeping body. (We all dream of what we do, so dream researchers' dreams are often about . . . well, dreams.) The bizarre premise of this particular dream was that four dimensions of the character's position each determined one dichotomy. Right or left denoted male versus female; above or beneath yielded good versus bad; in front or behind, powerful versus weak; ahead or behind in time, older versus younger. If located *exactly* where the dreamer slept, the character would appear as oneself. My mother, seated in front of me to my upper left, concluded, "Therefore there are seventeen possible dream characters." Now, the math is hardly complex, but on waking it did take me a moment of conscious reflection to confirm $2^4 + 1 = 17$, which my dreamed mother knew effortlessly. Somewhere outside of consciousness, my brain had performed the simple calculations. Accomplished mathematicians seem to be capable of their vastly more sophisticated level of math while dreaming also.

At the beginning of the twentieth century, psychologist

Edmond Mallet surveyed mathematicians about their dreams. Four reported ones in which a complete mathematical solution had arrived. Three of these concerned geometry problems. Eight respondents described having found the start of a solution or a useful idea in a dream. Fifteen said they had awakened with solutions or partial solutions, not knowing if these were linked to a dream or represented some other phenomena of sleep. All of the useful dreams recalled were highly visual.[13]

Harvard Professor Barry Mazur is noted for contributions to multiple areas of mathematics. His first major discovery was a method of solving certain complex topological problems by joining complex three-dimensional shapes to ones that complete them as spheres in infinite repetition. The technique has come to be known whimsically as "the Mazur swindle." The Committee of Sleep played a supporting role in its evolution.

"I'd already developed the strategy," Mazur told me, "but I was thinking of it as a possible step in one theorem I was trying to prove. I hadn't recognized that it was pointing to another group of problems. Anyone else looking over my shoulder could have seen that, but I was completely focused on the first problem." As Mazur was pondering the strategy, he dozed: "I was observing these shapes, seeing them glue onto each other to form a ball over and over in an infinite process. By this time it was so familiar that I didn't have to watch carefully. In this drowsing state, I finally realized it was saying something independent of the use I'd been trying to make of it."

Mazur applied his "swindle" to prove the generalized Schoen-flies Theorem—a famous topological problem. He was awarded the American Mathematical Society's 1965 Veblen Prize in

Geometry for this work. Other mathematicians have used it in related areas.

Mazur referred to the activity as "browsing." "Often as I go to sleep, mathematical issues are circling in front of me," he told me. "If it's a dream, it's the kind that's very closest to waking."

Other hypnagogic experiences aided Mazur's work, but he says, "I don't think dreams solve problems. I think they can help you realize that you have a solution. When you're working on a problem, there's a whole soup of stuff cooking. Things keep bubbling up to the surface of the cauldron. You've seen all the parts of the solution many times before—but not in the right light or they haven't cooked enough yet. A semi-awake browse over the problem can bring to the surface just the right combination and you say, 'My God—that's it!' "

Mazur is known for pointing out to other mathematicians that they have solved a problem before they've realized it, most notably Ken Ribet's contribution to the eventual proof of Fermat's last theorem. It may be that in complex mathematics, knowing that one has a solution is a more difficult step than for other endeavors we've discussed. But Mazur's cauldron metaphor also seems relevant to Agassiz and Loewi's reports in which recurring dreams seemed not to be working out solutions, but rather reminding the dreamer of what they'd forgotten the preceding night.

One major mathematician claimed that *all* his discoveries came to him in dreams. Srinivasa Ramanujan was remarkable in many ways. Widely regarded as the greatest mathematician India has ever produced, he had no formal university education. By 1913 the twenty-five-year-old clerk's theorems, written in his own odd notational system, so impressed local academics that they urged him to send his work to Professor G. H. Hardy at Cambridge University. The theorems telescoped many steps and lacked any Western concept of formal proof. Nevertheless, after poring over the puzzling hieroglyphics, Hardy saw their genius and invited Ramanujan to Cambridge. For five years the eccentric genius worked there, producing yet more astounding—if peculiar— theorems. Then the still young Ramanujan took ill and returned to India, where he died within two years. His work is still applied to areas as disparate as polymer chemistry and computer science.

And the source of these unique insights? Ramanujan said he owed all his mathematical discoveries to the Hindu goddess Namagiri, consort of the lion god Narasimha. He reported that Namagiri brought the mathematical insights in his dreams. His British collaborators were sadly uninterested in this source and recorded only that "Ramanujan said the goddess would bestow the insights in dreams," and "Namagiri would write the equations on his tongue."[14] About one dream, Ramanujan told them that a formula arrived by "seeing a hand write across a screen made red by flowing blood, tracing out elliptic integrals."[15]

It's difficult to reconstruct from these brief remarks the exact role of Ramanujan's dreams. As we'll find in Chapter 8, on cross-cultural issues, societies that treat dreams with reverence may foster more problem-solving dreams or better recall for them. On the other hand, they may also promote talk of "dreams" as a modest metaphor for one's creativity. Ramanujan clearly toiled long daytime hours over his notebooks of theorems. Obviously, this is when much of the work occurred. But Ramanujan stated several times that all of his theorems came in dreams. He took many mysteries to his early grave.

In 1899, Professor William Lamberton struggled with a more modest mathematical problem at the University of Pennsylvania. For two weeks he'd tried working it out through algebraic formulas, but eventually abandoned the task in frustration. "No thought of attempting a geometrical solution ever entered my head," he recalled.

A week after Lamberton gave up on the problem, he dreamed he was looking at a diagram depicting the solution—in wholly geometric terms. He awoke and opened his eyes, and the image persisted on a phantom blackboard across from his bed! He wrote of the experience: "I saw projected upon this blackboard surface a complete figure, containing not only the lines given by the problem but also a number of auxiliary lines and just such lines as without further thought solved the problem at once. . . . I sprang from bed and drew the figure on paper." [16]

The phenomenon of dream imagery superimposed onto the waking world for a short time after awakening is known as a "hypnagogic hallucination." This occurs when some of the physiological mechanisms of REM sleep persist after they would normally shut down. It's seen in people who have narcolepsy, a disease in which victims drop involuntarily and instantaneously into dreaming sleep at inopportune times, such as while driving a car. But studies also find that almost 5 percent of healthy people have experienced a hypnagogic hallucination at least once in their lives. Lamberton's solution highlights the propensity of mathematical and scientific problems for states of high brain activation in which dreaming and waking thought overlap. Hypnagogic dreams may be seen as the dreams closest to waking; hypnagogic hallucinations are dreams that persist *into* waking.

THE COMPUTER IN "SLEEP" MODE

Applied mathematical problems are also occasionally solved in dreams. Nicolas Condorcet, the eighteenth-century mathematician who first brought the calculus of probability to bear on social phenomena, dreamed the solution to one of his statistical problems without recording the details for posterity.[17] We can't know if Condorcet's probabilities were communicated to him visually, but all the examples I've encountered from the more modern field of computer science suggest that they likely were. Like statistics, the final product in computer programming is written in a defined notational system, but the key concepts may be represented visually.

Burke Nersesian is a programmer who has built a career writing financial planning software. At work recently on a program to track volatility of return on investment, he planned to compare the variation of predicted return with that of actual return. The resulting program displeased him. Then one night he had a dream: "I was seeing displays of graphs like the program would produce, only they were simpler," Nersesian told me. "In the dream, the program was basing the graphs solely on the unconditional value of the return, not using the predicted return at all. It was a paradox that the simpler version conveyed much more information than the complex one. I woke up and wrote the program the way I'd seen it in the dream." It was a far more efficient solution.

Physicist Stephen Bailey also does computer programming. One evening a friend of his, who taught statistics, described a program he needed to allocate computer memory to the complex matrices with which he worked. Bailey listened to a description of the problem, but wasn't planning to work on it.

That night, however, he had a dream: "The data was floating around in three-dimensional space. I was seeing abstract geometric shapes with numbers in them—floating, twisting, coming around to the arrangements in which they needed to be. At the same time, I knew what the algorithm had to be in order to achieve this. It would need to use a method called 'recursion' where you break a large problem into smaller problems repeatedly. All the details were in the dream. When I woke up, I went to my computer and did it just as in the dream—and it worked!" Bailey's experience wasn't isolated. "When I'm working on a project, I tend to dream about it. I'll even dream in computer language: C++ is what I use to program. More often, the dreams solve smaller parts of a problem." His dreams in the computer language C++ are rare examples—equivalent to the dreamed stanzas of poetry—in which the solution is not presented as a visual image or narrative, but rather in a mode that only the specialist would use in a dream. Bailey distinguishes these experiences from most of his other dreams. "Other times I have people, places, plot—these problem-solving dreams are much more focused."

Some computer dreams contain only the outlines of solutions. Canadian programmer Bill Markwick says, "The answer isn't neatly worked out. . . . Instead, it tends to be a concept or method of solution that I hadn't thought of while awake. It's as if some mysterious part of my brain handed up an algorithm and said, "Here, dolt, you do the figures—you're the one with a calculator."

Other dreams come complete with all details. In his research on lucid dreaming, Stephen LaBerge interviewed a computer scientist who learned to use lucidity reliably whenever he was stuck on a computer programming problem:

At night I will dream that I am sitting in a parlor (an old-fashioned one that Sherlock Holmes might use). I'm sitting with Einstein—white bushy hair—in the flesh. He and I are good friends. We talk about the program, start to do some flowcharts on a blackboard. Once we think we've come up with a good one, we laugh. Einstein says, "Well, the rest is history." Einstein excuses himself to go to bed. I sit in his recliner and doodle some code in a notepad. Then the code is all done. I look at it and say to myself, "I want to remember this flowchart when I wake up." I concentrate very hard on the blackboard and the notepad. Then I wake up. It is usually around 3:30 A.M. I get my flashlight (which is under my pillow), get my pencil and notepad (next to my bed), and start writing as fast as I can. I take this to work and usually it is 99 percent accurate.[18]

For decades, cognitive psychologists had studied creativity and problem solving in terms of consciously articulated processes. Philosopher Daniel Dennett calls this rational decision-making center the "command module" for personal identity. He points out that researchers have fallen into the fallacy that whatever is nonconscious must be not intelligent and "not me." Cognitive science is only recently recognizing a concept—long known to psychoanalysis—of an "intelligent unconscious," one with intentionality. With this trend comes a renewed interest in the neglected facility of intuition.

Seventy-two of eighty-three Nobel laureates surveyed recently strongly credited intuition in their success.[19] Konrad Lorenz (*Medicine* 1973) said, "If you press (only consciously) . . . nothing comes of it. You must give a sort of mysterious pressure and then rest, and suddenly BING! . . . the solution comes."

Neurologists tell us that intuition occurs when sensation or thinking is beneath the threshold of strength required for awareness of its source. Research in which subjects are shown slides for a fraction of a second—faster than we can consciously register— is employed as a paradigm for studying what happens in the brain during unconscious perception. When you flash a word (CAMEL, for example) at someone subliminally, they cannot report the word itself, but sometimes "guess" with great accuracy to what category it belongs (ANIMAL). Cambridge University psychologist Mark Price tells a story of testing a subject in such an experiment. The young man could not report the stimulus word or, on this occasion, its category, but he suddenly burst out laughing in the middle of the subsequent trial, explaining that an absurd fantasy about camels had just popped into his head.[20]

Brain-wave studies show that activation spreads from the original stimulus area. Although activity at the epicenter is too weak to enter consciousness, some associated concept primed from other of the days' activities may do so. Since much of our brain is devoted to visual imagery and narrative, these impressions often take the form of a picture or story—witness the camel. This is most true of dreaming because the visual areas of our brains are so extremely active then. This explains why dreamed solutions to scientific problems generated beneath conscious awareness are likely to appear visually. Narrative and interpersonal areas are also more active, so it makes sense that many insights are presented by dream characters (e.g., Albert Einstein or an Assyrian priest). In our next chapter, on inventions, dreams provide artists with new methods of engraving rather than simply the images to be engraved. Visual and personified aspects are again crucial—as is the intersection of waking and dreaming.

The "what if" component is intriguing in these scientific anecdotes. If Salvador Dalí had failed to recall one of his sea-urchin-induced visions, he might well have awakened and painted another image just as compelling. In the case of Fuselli, we wouldn't have had "The Nightmare," but perhaps an equivalent painting. It's hard to believe, however, that Kekulé would have founded a different branch of chemistry, or that Loewi would have performed an alternate Nobel Prize–winning experiment. Would they have eventually made the same discoveries in the waking state? Or would they never have done so? What if Margie Profet's cat hadn't awakened her? Might she, like Loewi and Agassiz, have repeated her dream the following night? Could the dream-maker be this capricious? We can't be sure of the answers to these questions—though we will revisit them in the final chapter, on controlled dream experiments. For now, let us simply be grateful that Profet's feline was a restless nocturnal hunter.

6

Of Sewing Machines and Other Dreams: Inventions of the Committee

With giant telescopes trained on distant points in the galaxy, Paul Horowitz is a real-life version of Jodie Foster's character in the film *Contact*. A Harvard physics professor, he's noted for his work in experimental physics. But his great passion is the search for extraterrestrial intelligence, or SETI. Horowitz builds the control mechanisms for telescopes used in experimental astrophysics and negotiates a fraction of the telescopes' stargazing time to search for signals from advanced life in other galaxies.

Most of his designs are radio telescopes, because radio signals travel great distances in a focused form more easily than light. By the fall of 1998, however, laser technology had developed far enough that Horowitz decided to design controls for an optical telescope to search for pulsed light signals. "There were literally an infinite number of ways we could put it together," he recalls. "It's not one big problem but lots of little ones. You figure out how to arrange one group of lenses, then you design a circuit to manipulate that. There were many stages where we would get blocked on how to do something."

And what would he do then?

> Often I'd have a dream. These problem-solving dreams are not like my others. I'm simply an observer. They have a lot of clarity—there's not the bizarreness of other dreams. These dreams have a narrator who's sketching the problem verbally. Then the voice is giving the solution. I'm also seeing the solution. I watch a man working on the mechanical device—arranging lenses for the optics or building the circuit—whatever it is that I'm stuck on at that point. The dream always takes it a slightly different way from what we've been trying [while] awake.
>
> I keep a pencil and paper next to the bed to write down these dreams. That's the one way in which they are like other dreams—they're beads of moisture on a very hot stove. They'll evaporate in a second if I don't get them down. I take my notes into work and tell my team, "I've dreamed up a solution—literally." They've gotten quite used to doing things based on my dreams.

On the laser telescope, Horowitz says he had at least three dreams about assembling optics and at least two about circuits—always visual aspects of the problems. He's had similar dream series when working on radio telescope projects. They always occur in the middle of the night, after several hours of sleep. They overlap waking thought only in their clarity and degree of logic—he does not seem to be dozing like the dreamers in the preceding chapter.

With the last chapter's examples of Einstein and other dream mentors in mind, I asked Horowitz if the narrator or the man he sees building telescopes reminds him of anyone. "I guess they're both most like me," he says. "The voice sounds like mine and the man looks a lot like me. But I don't think this during the dream. I'm just observing the solution."

Like Horowitz's telescopes, many other man-made devices have first functioned in a dream. Most appear at a point when the inventor has worked out much of the design while awake, yet is stuck on one crucial detail, which the dream delivers. Inventors as a group may be especially likely to get help from the Committee because of the nature of their problems. They usually need bold solutions to problems that are partly visual or spatial. As with Horowitz, many of their dreams come from sound sleep rather than the dozing wherein so many mathematical and chemical formulas arise. This may be because the visual images needed are more typical of those in dreaming. Nevertheless, these dreams are often remarkably focused and realistic, as we've seen in the case of Horowitz. Even when they're more metaphoric, they come to a talented person who has been puzzling over a problem and is often under pressure for a solution.

One of the most fanciful examples of invention dreams also deals with lasers. For years, Allen Huang, head of AT&T Bell Laboratories' optical computing research department, worked on creating a computer using optical laser circuits rather than electrical ones, but he was stuck on designing the specific circuitry. None of the models from conventional computing worked. Repeatedly, Huang dreamed of two opposing armies of sorcerer's apprentices who carried pails of data toward each other, but always stopped short of colliding. Then, one night, the armies passed *through* each other. To Huang, they were like light passing through light.

The dream told him that because laser beams could pass through each other, unlike electric currents, they didn't need their own pathways. "Then I knew," Huang says, "there was a way." He has since proven that lasers can function in a new type of computer that ignores conventional rules of circuitry. Huang believes in listening to the unconscious. "Too often," he observes, "we are shamed into not going with our instincts."[1]

Perhaps lasers are heavily represented among invention dreams because they are both cutting-edge technology and lend themselves to visual imagery. Even though Huang's dream differs from Horowitz's in many ways, they were both working on problems having visual representations, were stuck in their waking work, and dreamed in deep sleep rather than while dozing.

THE TURTLE BOAT

Perhaps the oldest recorded example of a dreamed invention is the Korean armored "turtle boat." This invention is four hundred years old and shrouded in myth. However, several facts are clear: Admiral Yi Sun-shin was the commander of Korea's navy during the 1592–98 invasion by Japanese naval forces. At first the larger Japanese navy dominated the conflict. Admiral Yi was worrying about how he could repel their ships when he fell asleep one night and dreamed:

> I go out to sea to look for food to feed my sailors, who are exhausted after several battles. No matter how far I sail

my ship, I can't find anything. Suddenly a huge turtle emerges from the sea. I try to capture it for food and use all my arrows and other weapons. Despite tremendous efforts, I can't get the turtle into my hand. Moreover, fire is poring out of its mouth, which frightens me terribly.[2]

Waking in surprise, Yi immediately conceived the idea of a very special vessel, the *kobukson,* Korean for "turtle boat."

Shaped like a turtle, the ship was built of thick wood blocks and covered with stout iron armor. It was in fact the world's first ironclad battleship. It also had a turtle's belly—a circular, flat bottom in contrast to the more streamlined traditional boats. This shape allowed the *kobukson* to gyrate freely, nimbly ramming and sinking Japanese ships. The ship's prow was shaped like a dragon's head, through which a cannon fired and sulfurous smoke billowed. Six cannon were concealed behind the armor on each ship so that soldiers could fire from a protected vantage. Even the ship's metal tail held a cannon.[3] The powerful arms almost literally spewed fire.

At the time, the Japanese army was superior at hand-to-hand fighting as a result of the many internal battles of their "Warring States Period." In sea battles, Japanese ships would close with enemy ships, and soldiers would swarm aboard and engage in deadly hand-to-hand fighting. It was the highest honor to be designated as the first person allowed to board an enemy ship. But the top of the *kobukson* was covered with lethal pikes and swords. Jumping onto it was certain death.

Days after the first *kobukson* were completed, the 200,000-strong Japanese army boarded seven hundred warships to cross the sea for what they thought would be their final invasion of Korea.

Korean lore holds that the first time the Japanese forces encountered the *kobukson,* they were terrified, thinking that the fire-spouting ship was a deadly sea monster. In any case, once they were familiar with its real nature and capabilities, they ran away whenever they spotted it, seeing there was no hope of winning a battle against it. Admiral Yi's dreams and turtle boats had repelled the Japanese invasion.

FROM SEWING MACHINES TO ANTIAIRCRAFT GUNS

In Western culture, dream inventions go back as far as the Committee's contributions to art and literature. In fact, one of the same visionary geniuses who bridged those two fields gives us one of the early inventions. William Blake, whose dreamed paintings we discussed in Chapter 1 and whose poetry is examined in Chapter 3, also dreamed of a process by which he could reproduce this art and literature in quantity for sale. Blake was short of money and searching for a means to self-publish his combined sketches and verse in a manner that would be handsome but not costly. He had a dream in which his dead brother Robert gave him detailed instructions for chemically etching images onto metal plates. It was ingeniously suited to the reproduction of both art and text. The next day Blake sent his wife out to buy all the—happily inexpensive—materials with their last half-crown. The dream method worked beautifully and the resulting book, *Songs,* sold well.[4]

Similarly, in *The Mystery of Dreams,* William Stevens recounts his scientist brother-in-law struggling with the problem of how to etch a design into the steel blade of a knife. He spent many waking hours on this question—to no avail. Then one night he dreamed straightforwardly of a chemical process that achieved this, and recalled it clearly upon awakening.[5]

Learning to use metals effectively was as major an issue in early inventions as laser technology is today. This theme is reflected in yet a fourth of the Committee's offerings to Western invention. Until 1782, gunshot was made by a laborious process of hammering lead nuggets into spheres, one at a time. William Watt was a plumber who was familiar with the manufacture of gunshot. He also worked with lead in making pipes. One night he dreamed he was in a storm, being pelted by raindrops of molten lead. He awoke puzzled by the dream. Over the next several nights he had the same dream twice more. Finally, on the third repetition, Watt—familiar with the way that molten lead formed balls in water—realized that the falling spheres were exactly the size and shape needed for gunshot. His dreaming mind had invented the process that revolutionized the way gunshot was made—dropping molten lead into water, where the drops cooled readily into perfect spheres.[6]

In 1844, Elias Howe had begun to design the prototype of a sewing machine, but couldn't figure out how the machine was to hold a needle. His needles still had their hole at the end opposite the point, like regular hand-sewing needles. He could find no way for the machine to secure them that didn't interfere with passing the needle through fabric.

One night Howe dreamed he was captured by savages in warpaint, who threatened to kill him if he didn't finish the machine right away.

> Cold sweat poured down his brow, his hands shook with fear, his knees quaked. Try as he would, the inventor could not get the missing figure in the problem over

which he had worked so long. All this was so real to him that he cried aloud. In the vision he saw himself surrounded by dark-skinned and painted warriors, who formed a hollow square about him and led him to the place of execution. Suddenly he noticed that near the heads of the spears which his guards carried, there were eye-shaped holes. He had solved the secret! What was needed was a needle with an eye near the point! He awoke from his dream, sprang out of bed, and at once made a whittled model of the eye-pointed needle, with which he brought his experiments to a successful close.[7]

Howe's is one of the more fanciful invention dreams, complete with many of dreaming's typical distortions. His anxiety about not completing the project was blown up into the threat of death. The needles had grown into giant spears. But the Committee still makes its "point" quite clearly. It announces the dream is about the construction of the sewing machine. The meaning of the holes at the tips is more readily obvious than Watt's rain of metal.

The dream that led to the invention of the first computer-controlled antiaircraft gun was yet more straightforward. In 1940 the Nazis were ravaging Holland and Belgium. J. B. Parkinson was a young engineer at Bell Labs who had just developed a computer-controlled potentiometer to improve the accuracy with which telephone transmissions were measured. Like most Americans, he was worried about the news from Europe when he had the following dream:

I found myself in a gun pit with an anti-aircraft crew. . . . The men were Dutch or Belgian by their uniforms.

There was a gun there . . . and the impressive thing was that every shot brought down an airplane. After three or four shots, one of the men in the crew smiled at me and beckoned me to come closer to the gun. When I drew near, he pointed to the exposed end of the left trunnion. Mounted there was the control potentiometer of my level recorder. There was no mistaking it—it was the identical item.[8]

Upon awaking, Parkinson realized that "if the potentiometer could control the high-speed motion of a recoding pen with great accuracy, why couldn't a suitably engineered device do the same thing for an antiaircraft gun?" The military built Parkinson's device and dubbed it the M-9. In August 1944, the Germans launched ninety-one bombers from the Antwerp area; M-9 guns shot down eighty-nine of them.

On a more domestic note, Luther Burbank's work in the early twentieth century earned him the reputation as the all-time greatest plant breeder. Burbank developed many new varieties of fruits, vegetables, and flowers, including the Burbank potato and the Shasta daisy. He never mentioned dreams in his own three books; however, Burbank's secretary Mildred Hirschberg reported that he wrote all of his down. As they occurred through the night, he jotted them down telegraphically on bits of scrap paper and tossed them to the floor as he returned to sleep. Mrs. Hirschberg was assigned the task of going through his quarters, gathering these up each day, and typing out their contents. She reported that they looked like "mostly nonsense" to her, but Burbank studied them carefully and said that many of his best plant ideas came from them.[9]

THE COMMITTEE TAKES ON HOUDINI

Some inventions of the Committee are not devices—nor daisies—but systems for doing things that have visual-spatial components. For years, Dmitri Mendeleyev struggled to find a way to classify chemical elements by such traits as their atomic weight and valence. He had drafted several tables that achieved this to varying degrees but was not completely satisfied with any of them. One night after working on the problem, he fell asleep and "saw in a dream a table where all the elements fell into place as required." Immediately he made a waking record of what he'd seen. He found that "only in one place did a correction later seem necessary." The table of his dream is now the "Periodic Table of the Elements," which every beginning chemistry or physics student studies to this day.[10]

The Committee rewarded equally directly a more frivolous pursuit of M. Jeffrey Rosen's. Rosen is now CEO of Liberty Publishing, but in high school he worked part-time as a magician. Rosen's best friend, also a magic buff, saw a show featuring a magician who was one of the few in the world who could perform Houdini's famous Dissolving Cards trick. Rosen's buddy returned from the show baffled and described the "impossible" feat to him in detail.

In this illusion, the magician shuffles a deck of cards. A volunteer assistant inspects the deck and counts out fifteen cards, seals them in an envelope, and lays the envelope in plain sight on a table to one side of the stage. Then the assistant counts out another fifteen cards. The assistant takes this second set of cards into the audience. Three people in turn choose a card. Their selections are read and recorded before being sealed in another envelope with the rest of this second set of fifteen cards. This envelope is laid on a table on the opposite side of the stage. The magician—who has not touched the cards since the shuffling—announces that he will "dissolve" the chosen cards in the second envelope and make them reappear with the first group. He gestures from afar to "draw" the cards from one envelope to the other. Then the audience assistant opens each envelope. The second envelope now has just twelve cards in it. The first one now contains eighteen cards—the three chosen ones sit on top of the others.

This is the most mysterious trick Houdini ever devised, and he took its secret to the grave with him. "I made my friend describe it over and over," Rosen recalls. "We didn't see how it could possibly be done without the helpers being plants in the audience—yet this was anathema to Houdini or to any serious magicians attempting to reconstruct his performance. We spent weeks trying to figure out the trick." Then Rosen had a dream, much in the format of Horowitz's, in which a magician was performing the trick. "As I witnessed it, a voice was telling me how it was done. And I could see exactly how and why it must work! I just stared in amazement. The concept was so simple, but it worked only when the execution and timing were flawless. I awoke with no question in my mind that this was what the magician my friend had watched—and indeed Houdini—had done."

Rosen practiced and practiced the trick's precise timing until he had mastered it. He worked his way through college entirely on earnings from magic. Eventually he was able to confirm that his dreamed method was indeed the one that select initiates were using. "Now it's been written about in texts for magic," says

Rosen, "but when I was in high school it wasn't published—it was a well-guarded secret." However, Rosen still declined to clue in a layperson to the secret the Committee and magicians share.

A similar and equally literal solution to a problem appeared in the Marquis Hervey de Saint-Denys's book *Dreams and How to Guide Them,* where he recorded a friend's solution to a chess problem. He'd been working on how to reach checkmate in six moves from an unusual position: "He dreamed that he had the chessboard in front of him, with each piece in its correct place. He continued his study of the problem, but this time the solution he was looking for appeared with marvelous lucidity. The game was continued and ended, and he clearly saw the disposition of the pieces on the board after each move."[11]

Leaping from bed, he went to the chessboard and played the six moves from memory, finding that they were correct!

PETITIONING THE COMMITTEE FOR HELP

Many of the dreamers thus far in this book say they never knew a solution could arrive in a dream. Others have heard of one or two famous examples. Margie Profet and Paul Horowitz both learned about Kekulé in school. But what happens when people familiar with many such examples actually petition the Committee for help in solving problems?

One such dreamer is Floyd Ragsdale. An engineer at Du Pont, he took the creativity workshop they offered to employees. The workshop included the idea of dreaming solutions to practical problems and outlined the famous examples of Kekulé and Howe.

Leaders encouraged Ragsdale to write down his dreams about work and examine them for potential help with ongoing problems.

At the outbreak of the Gulf War, the Pentagon asked Du Pont to step up production of Kevlar fiber, which was used in troops' bulletproof vests. Du Pont turned out large quantities quickly until a machine broke down. This malfunction was costing seven hundred dollars a minute for the company and threatening thousands of soldiers' lives. Ragsdale was one of many engineers Du Pont assigned to fix the machine. None of them could even locate the problem.

Exhausted by the effort, Ragsdale lay down in bed one night, still pondering the problem. He fell asleep and dreamed he was part of the piece of equipment. He saw springs and hoses and water spraying everywhere. Water ran outside of the machine. He woke up and wrote down simply "hoses, springs." Puzzling over the notation and the dream, he had a "Eureka!" experience. The hoses must be closing down, he realized, blocking the flow of water and stopping the functioning of the whole machine. And what would keep them open? Coiled springs inside them!

The next morning, Ragsdale sought out his supervisor, identified the problem, and proposed his solution. His supervisor was dubious even without knowing that the source of this insight was a dream. No one had fingered the hoses as the problem. Only later during the day, in a "try everything" mode, did the team pull off a hose and find that indeed it had collapsed—which couldn't be detected from the outside. The supervisor then allowed Ragsdale to fit the hoses with springs, and the machine was up and running at the end of the day. That one dream saved Du Pont between three and four million dollars and the U.S. military numerous lives.[12]

THE RULES OF DREAM INCUBATION

Psychologists have developed "incubation" rituals to encourage problem-solving dreams. These usually target interpersonal and emotional problems, but they are also relevant to objective creative tasks. Incubation instructions usually include the following:

1. Write down the problem as a brief phrase or sentence, and place this by your bed.
2. Review the problem for a few minutes just before going to bed.
3. Once in bed, visualize the problem as a concrete image if it lends itself to this. Visualize yourself dreaming about the problem, awakening, and writing on the bedside note pad.
4. Tell yourself you want to dream about the problem just as you are drifting off to sleep.
5. Keep a pen and paper—perhaps also a flashlight or pen with a lighted tip—on the night table.
6. Arrange objects connected to the problem on your night table (Howe could have used sewing needles and fabric) or on the wall across from your bed if they lend themselves to a poster (Blake could have tacked up his sketches and poems).
7. Upon awakening, lie quietly before getting out of bed. Note whether there is any trace of a recalled dream, and invite more of the dream to return if possible. Write it down.

One dream psychologist who applies such techniques full-time is Anjali Hazarika of India's National Petroleum Management Program. Hazarika runs creativity workshops much like Du

Pont's, but focuses exclusively on dreaming. Small groups of oil executives and engineers gather for three days of instruction and experiential exercises with her. Hazarika emphasizes solving personal problems at home that are interfering with job performance and helping work groups get along better with each other through dream insights. However, some of her workshop participants choose to focus on objective problems.

Hazarika told me of one chemist who was developing enzymes that would refine crude oil. He asked the Committee of Sleep for help with this. That night he dreamed he was next to a road when a big truck rumbled by with a load of rotten cabbages. He could see them heaped over the top of the truck, and he could smell their stench as they passed by. It was a vivid dream, but when he told it in the group, neither he nor anyone else could make sense of it. Hazarika tried to help him interpret it, and other members of the group offered symbolic associations to cabbages and rot, but they didn't get far.

The next Monday, when the chemist returned to his lab to work on his oil-refinement project, he suddenly realized the dream was literally true. As cabbages decomposed, bacteria would break them down into exactly the kind of enzymes he sought! And cabbages were dirt-cheap—rotten ones were simply thrown out. He proceeded to develop a technique for crude-oil refinement using exactly the material his dream had trucked in for him.

A petroleum engineer in another of Hazarika's groups was working to improve a device used for pumping oil from the wells. An S-shaped tube coming out of the pump kept clogging, and the machine had to be repeatedly stopped and cleaned. He incubated a dream about this and saw the letter S changing into a U.

He woke and realized the pipe could have one gentle curve and still get the oil to where it was needed. His new design did not clog as the old one had.[13]

In Chapter 9 we'll discuss promising laboratory research on dream incubation. These modern findings echo what the inventors of the last several centuries have stumbled onto for themselves—but take them further. First, however, we will examine a still older dream tradition—the original focus of dream incubation for the ancients—that of medical diagnosis and healing.

7

THE CLAW OF THE PANTHER:

DREAMS AND THE BODY

An Englishman dreamed that he, his wife, and three children were traveling on horseback. The ride was pleasant until he spotted two black panthers crouched in the bushes beside the trail. He persuaded his wife and children to gallop away, while he brought up the rear himself to guard them from danger. The panthers gave chase, and gained on the dreamer. One leaped at his back, its claw piercing him just to the left of his spine between his shoulder blades. In pain, he shook the great cat off and galloped on. Ahead, his family had reached the safety of a small town, where several men stood waiting in white coats. As he galloped up, the men in white waved mysterious objects at the panthers, frightening them off. The dreamer felt relief, but the last departing panther looked back over its shoulder with a final menacing glare.

The Englishman recounted the dream to his therapist. Neither could make much of it. Two months later, while the man was shaving, his wife noticed a striking mole between his shoulder blades, just to the left of his spine. A biopsy revealed it to be a malignant melanoma. The word *melanoma* is derived from the Latin *mela*, meaning black. Surgery removed the cancer. The dreamer had no family history of the disease, and had never been badly sunburned. Healthy so far, he reflected, "Given the highly metastatic nature of melanomas, I sometimes think of the panther's parting glance." After diagnosis, this man's central concern was protecting his family from the effects of his illness—just as he'd focused on protecting them from the panthers in the dream.[1]

FROM THE TEMPLES OF ASCLEPIUS TO THE EXAMINING ROOM OF HIPPOCRATES: MEDICAL DREAMS THROUGH HISTORY

Dreams in this chapter may sound at first like bizarre coincidences or claims for the paranormal. But they do relate to the problem solving we've discussed so far. As with other cognitive processes, body sensations and our reflections about them may first reach our consciousness in a dream. Recall the visual stimuli experiments described in Chapter 5, in which a man who never consciously perceived the word *camel* had a comic fantasy about camels. The Englishman may have subconsciously glimpsed a growth on his back or felt nerve sensations from his mole too subtle to register on his waking mind. Some dreams recounted in this chapter alerted the dreamer to such a stimulus. Some diagnosed the sensation. Still others presented ideas about treating it.

British psychologist Robin Royston heard the panther example in 1994, but the concept of dreams reflecting one's physical state has been known since the dawn of civilization. Aristotle wrote, "Beginnings of diseases and other distempers which are about to visit the body . . . must be more evident in the sleeping than in the waking state."[2]

The ancient Greeks worshiped a god of healing, Asclepius, son of Apollo. Legend held that Asclepius was trained in medicine by the centaur Chiron. The sick traveled to his temples to sleep amid statues of Asclepius while the floor crawled with snakes, his sacred helpers. This is why the caduceus, the symbol of medicine, features two snakes climbing a staff. If the supplicant was worthy, the god appeared in a dream and told the nature of the illness or prescribed a remedy.

Greek physicians endorsed these religious beliefs, yet offered physiologic explanations for most diagnostic dreams. Hippocrates speculated that we withdraw attention from the external world and focus on the body during sleep. Galen, the second-century c.e. Greek physician who pioneered our Western diagnostic system, wrote a treatise titled *Prophecy in Dreams*. He hailed dreams as a major source of diagnostic and treatment information. Patients on the verge of sweating off a fever dreamt of bathing or swimming in pools of hot water, Galen said, "the same way the thirsty dream of gulping water or the hungry of feasting." He taught that dreams of rivers often referred to circulation of blood: flooding banks signaled excessive blood pressure, dry river beds a dangerously low one.

Galen had his own encounters with Asclepius. At the age of twenty he became critically ill, but dreamed the god appeared and ordered him to cut and bleed the artery in his hand between his thumb and first finger. Galen followed the directive and credited it with saving his life. Bleeding was a common medical procedure in those days. Its only real benefit in terms of modern medical understanding would have been as a crude way to lower blood pressure. When Galen was thirty-eight, Asclepius appeared to him again, forbidding him to go to war with the emperor Marcus Aurelius. It's easy to see how this directive aided his health!

These dreams were the exception; Galen attributed most examples in his book to physical rather than divine origins. "Someone dreamt that one of his legs turned into stone," he recounted. "This dream was interpreted by many skilled in these matters as a reference to the man's slaves. However, contrary to all of our expectations, the dreamer became paralyzed in that leg."[3] Hippocrates wrote of a similar instance of a dream about injury to the legs indicating a problem with them.[4] Both ancient physicians discussed how hard it is to distinguish somatic from metaphoric dreams. Modern dream interpreters still struggle with this issue—though they no longer have to consider slave management as an alternate explanation.

The Man who Mistook Sigmund Freud for His Head: Modern Takes on Medical Dreams from Jung to Sacks

We remember Carl Jung for his psychological interpretations of dreams, but he also noted their somatic dimension. One follower submitted a dream to Jung from an epileptic patient and was surprised when Jung commented, without knowing the man's diagnosis, "The dream to which you refer was very clearly a representation of an organic disorder."[5] Jung tells of another dream that led him to correctly diagnose progressive muscular dystrophy in a young girl he'd first assumed to be suffering from hysteria.[6]

Existential psychotherapist Medard Boss also described dreams that sensed illnesses that did not yet show physical symptoms. A young woman dreamed that a Balinese demon forced her to sit on a central heating pipe, causing burning pain between her legs. Boss pointed out that Freudians would have a simple interpretation of this—but it would be wrong. After three nights of this dream, the young woman developed actual physical pain and was diagnosed with acute cystitis.

Another young woman told Boss of recurring dreams that her family members turned into stone statues. After four of these dreams, she developed severe catatonic schizophrenia, and her whole body became frozen with rigidity.[7] Similarly, in Patricia Garfield's book, *The Healing Power of Dreams*, she describes an elderly patient who dreamed of characters who were ominously still. In one dream, seated figures in a kitchen seemed to be wax-work. In another, corpses sat upright in an undertaker's parlor. After several months of such dreams, this woman was discovered unconscious. Her diagnosis was myxedema coma—a potentially fatal slowing of metabolism due to an underactive thyroid gland.[8] Most of these examples are neurological. Because dreams occur in the brain, its disorders would be likely to shape dream content.

The neurologist Oliver Sacks has recorded the dreams of patients for almost every illness he's treated. One patient whose circulation was cut off by an overly tight cast dreamed of a six-trillion-ton "neutonium man" sitting on his leg. Sacks's Tourette's patients has "Touretty" dreams—wild, fast, and full of unexpected, tangential actions.

Sacks had just begun his career when he first noticed the relationship of dreams to symptoms in a migraine clinic. There the mosaic patterns and zigzagging lines of the headaches' visual symptoms, called *auras*, showed up as fireworks and other imagery blended into the patients' dreams. When Sacks later worked with epileptics, one patient told him of a dream of being in court. The prosecutor was Sigmund Freud, who banged on the dreamer's head with a gavel, but the blows registered in his left arm. The patient awoke to find himself having a motor seizure. It had begun with pounding signals in the brain, which produced violent contractions in his arm.[9]

In his book *Awakenings*, Sacks wrote of a number of sleeping-sickness patients. Before her illness, one dreamed of being imprisoned in a remote castle, becoming a statue of stone inside a world frozen in stillness. Another patient had a nightmare of swaying wildly, dropping everything she picked up. The very next day she developed an acute sensory neuropathy with exactly these symptoms. Parkinson's disease showed up first in one patient's dreams of being frozen, of rushing and being unable to stop, and of time "changing scale." These dreams continued for months before symptoms developed in waking life.

Cancer is one of the most common modern illnesses. Tumors produce pressure on nerves and other somatic stimuli that only slowly reach consciousness, but that we may sense subliminally before then. Malignant growths also activate the immune system even when its efforts are futile. Researchers now know immunology to be deeply integrated with the nervous system. Therefore it's not surprising that cancer generates many warning dreams.

Yale physician Bernie Siegel writes of a journalist who dreamed that torturers placed hot coals beneath his chin. He felt heat sear his throat, and screamed in desperation as the coals gnawed his larynx. When telling his girlfriend the dream, he wondered aloud if he might have throat cancer. Soon after, he had another dream of a group of medicine men encircling him, sticking hypodermics in what they called his "neck brain." Within a few months he began to have symptoms in that area. His doctor initially told him nothing was wrong. The dreamer insisted on further tests. These found cancer in his thyroid.

A breast cancer patient of Siegel's dreamed that her head was shaved and the word *cancer* was written on it. There had been no signs in her brain yet, but three weeks later a scan showed metastasized tumors there.[10]

Physician and analyst Daniel Schneider described patients whose dreams also seemed to warn of cancer. One smoker felt machine-gun fire cutting him methodically in half, beginning from the left side of his chest. A checkup revealed cancer in the lower left lobe of his lung, not yet metastasized. Another patient of Schneider's, who had an undetected but swiftly metastasizing neoplasm of his gallbladder, dreamed of his body "exploding, shattering into a thousand fragments."[11]

In most of these anecdotes, only in hindsight did the physician or patient believe the dreaming mind was signaling the presence of cancer. Even Siegel's journalist who worried he might have throat cancer sought no help until his waking symptoms appeared. But once in a while someone takes to heart the Committee's message upon its arrival. Let's examine two such dreamers in detail, with their comments on why dreams captured their attention.

Psychologist Shanee Stepakoff credits her early detection and cure of melanoma to a series of dreams. In the fall of 1996, Stepakoff noticed a light spot on her face and went to her doctor, who said it was an age spot. Consciously reassured, she nevertheless began to have anxiety dreams. At first the topics were obscure: in one dream she is going to a "terminal" place—but the word referred to an airport. In another she's warned she doesn't have a "regulator." Cancer is defined as "unregulated cell growth," but the dream phrase referred to scuba equipment. In a third, Stepakoff learned that "a person can just be walking down the street and disappear."

The next dream mentioned cancer directly. Her mentor appeared and told Stepakoff that she (the mentor) had cancer. Stepakoff associated this with the spot on her face and decided to get it checked again in two months when her new health insurance would take effect. Then she had the most vivid dream of her life. A man told her she had a rare window of opportunity— overtly, this referred to a class she must use a "check" for. The character used the word "check" eight times in reference to money. But then he broke out of the context of the class and told Stepakoff she needed to get "checked for cancer—soon."

Stepakoff made another dermatology appointment that day, even though this involved writing a *check* she knew would bounce. This doctor also judged it to be an ordinary age spot. At Stepakoff's insistence, he reluctantly agreed to biopsy it. The results came back as melanoma in the epidermis—where it is usually curable with surgery. It had grown right to the border of the dermis, where it usually progresses to fatal metastases elsewhere in the body, but no cells had invaded that area yet. Stepakoff had just made her "window of opportunity." Her early-stage melanoma was removed with a low chance of recurrence. If she had waited in accordance with her doctors' waking advice, her prognosis would have been grim.

"I don't pretend to know how such things work," Stepakoff told me, "but I think my unconscious knew something was wrong. I was keeping a dream journal at that time, typing my dreams in every day. I couldn't just ignore my dream the way most people do at most times in their life." [12]

Another dreamer who took a medical dream seriously was Nancy Parsifal, a writer and teacher, and mother of one son, Cyrus. Parsifal told me the story of his birth:

> When I was three months pregnant, I started bleeding. I didn't lose the baby and they couldn't find anything wrong. I worried about it and told the doctor I wanted natural childbirth. He said, "Oh, what we do is completely natural, we just give a little something called a spinal to relieve the pain toward the end." This didn't sound natural to me, but I was so naïve and meek that I just said, "Okay, if that's the way it's done . . ."
>
> That night I had a dream that I was in labor. They gave me the spinal and I gave birth to a baby boy. He was very blue when he was born. He turned gray and died. Then I turned gray and died.
>
> I've always paid a lot of attention to my dreams. But this one was completely different than my others in tone—there was a clarity. I just knew it wasn't like my years of dream journals. I didn't just listen because it was scary—it was *real*.
>
> I went back to my doctor and told him the dream. He said pregnant women have a lot of silly dreams. I said I'd have to find another doctor if he wouldn't do natural childbirth. He was still saying this stuff about spinals being natural.
>
> I did locate a doctor who was agreeable to doing a natural delivery. I told him the dream and he seemed interested. We got along well and I got him to write a "no meds" order in my hospital chart. I had more bleed-

ing at six months, but again nothing was found to be wrong.

Then, six weeks early, I woke up in the middle of the night. I was all wet and thought my water had broken. But when I got up and turned on the light, I was standing in a huge pool of blood. My husband got me to the hospital and the baby was coming. There was just a resident on call. I pointed out the "no meds" order, but he wanted to give me a muscle relaxant that he said would make the delivery easier. I kept saying no. My husband argued with me, saying the doctor must know best. I was trying to get them to find my obstetrician, but it was the middle of the night and they weren't calling. So my baby, Cyrus, was delivered by the resident with me still refusing medication. He was very blue and the cord was wrapped around his neck several times. He wasn't breathing. They rushed him out of the delivery room. The charge nurse teared up and said, "I wish it could be different, but they'll do everything they can to save him."

Much later, the resident came back to say Cyrus was breathing and stable in intensive care. He had a skull fracture, his heart was enlarged so his lungs couldn't expand fully, and he had an extra digit space between his toes. It turned out I'd had a huge fibroid cyst they hadn't detected that was pressing on him the whole time in the womb.

Then the resident amazed me by saying he wanted to apologize about the medication. "If we'd given you a relaxant, it would have slowed his heartbeat even more," he told me. "He never would have survived."

My own doctor took over, and Cyrus was in intensive

care for weeks. Everything got better: his skull closed properly, his heart got stronger, and his lungs expanded. The staff called him the "miracle baby." The only thing that was still worrying them was the extra digit space between his toes, because that's often indicative of mental retardation. So far there was no sign of that, but it was too early to tell for sure. Then my doctor told *me* a dream. He (the doctor) was lying on the delivery table with a bunch of people gathered around him. He pointed to his foot and said "Look, I have an extra digit space between *my* toes—and *I'm* okay."

I just knew that was his intuition sensing that Cyrus would be all right.

Cyrus is currently a healthy, bright college junior. "I was such a shy, meek person back then," Nancy Parsifal recalls. "It took something as dramatic as that dream to make me disagree with a male authority figure."

Some would say this type of dream represents a simple coincidence. Parsifal's first physician was not wrong in suggesting that pregnant women often have anxiety dreams about their unborn children. Any of us may worry about cancer or symbolize other concerns as that dramatic ailment. If the nightmare doesn't come true, few of us recall and retell the anecdote. So how do we know that a dreamed correspondence is not just metaphoric anxiety combined with coincidence?

We don't know for sure, and some fraction of our anxious dreams probably are in fact exactly that. But it is a fact that our bodies can sense more than reaches our consciousness. Dreams can convey subliminal perceptions, so at least some of these may be real warnings from our sleeping minds. In waking life, we know that a sensation may mean nothing. When we have such a waking perception—or intuition of illness—we do well to check it out, though some of these instances will be false alarms. The same is true of body dreams: many will turn out to be groundless, but why miss the ones that *are* important?

RESEARCH STUDIES

Most stories of dreams warning of illness are anecdotal. But there is some research on the topic. Are these dreams more common in illness? What signs are most likely to occur during physical illness rather than with metaphoric concerns?

The largest study so far was done in Russia. Researcher Vasilii Kasatkin amassed a collection of 1,642 dreams from 247 patients and tracked their medical condition. He found that repeated dreams of wounds were the strongest predictors of impending illness. These dreams were longer and more intense than ones reflecting ordinary stresses. They often persisted through the night and recurred on subsequent nights.

The area of injury in the dream was usually the same as the developing illness. An ulcer patient dreamed he was eating pizza and his stomach "broke open." Another dreamed about a rat gnawing at the lower right part of his abdomen where his ulcer was later found. Yet another patient dreamed of dogs tearing at his stomach before being diagnosed with stomach cancer. A woman whose father had suffered from epilepsy dreamed that he took a tight vise off his own head and placed it on hers just hours before she had the first seizure of her life.

Dreams of chest wounds among Kasatkin's patients generally preceded heart attacks. Dreams of lower abdominal injury occured in early liver or kidney disease.[13]

Developing illness produced a high rate of distress dreams among Kasatkin's patients, though many did not refer to the specific body area affected. Ninety-one percent of the dreams of patients with undiagnosed illness were described as "frightening." Also common was imagery of blood, corpses, tombs, war, raw meat, and dirty water. There were many dream references to hospitals, doctors, and medicines. Because dreams often appeared before the first overt symptom, Kasatkin advocates routinely including dreams in medical diagnosis. "By correctly interpreting dreams, we've been able to discover and treat serious illnesses long before they would be diagnosed by any traditional means," he reports. "We have been able to save many lives."[14]

We will see in the next chapter that shamans routinely have problem-solving dreams about their patients. But in Western medicine most dreams—even physicians'—reflect the dreamer's own body. The experience of Parsifal's physician is rare. Kasatkin interviewed one doctor who dreamed of his patient being attacked by muggers. They cut out his right kidney and left it lying on the ground. It was the physician's right kidney, however, that soon turned out to be badly infected. A medical student in Kasatkin's study dreamed she was lying on the earth when it gave way, falling on her and compressing her chest. Although this could have referred simply to her job caring for tuberculosis patients, two months later she learned she had caught the disease herself while working there.[15]

In the United States, physician Robert Smith studied forty-nine patients with heart problems and correlated the severity of their illness with dream content. He found that men with the worst cardiac function had more dreams about death, while affected women had more involving separation. Smith concluded that in at least some cases, "these dreams had a warning function, signaling the presence of severe biological impairment. If a useful intervention occurred as a result of these warnings, the dreams would have an adaptive meaning or function." [16]

Jungian analyst Robbie Bosnak led a dream group for patients with heart transplants. He wrote of this in a 1996 book I edited, *Trauma and Dreams*. Bosnak found that postsurgical dreams not only portrayed psychological issues, but also predicted which patients were likely to reject their new organs. Those with the best long-term outcomes had dreams with symbolism of incorporating the new heart, such as one who dreamed of accepting the gift of a beautiful rose from the deceased donor. [17]

CHARACTERISTICS OF MEDICAL DREAMS

A question arises about these examples: Why are they so metaphoric, while the dreams in chapters on science and inventions are often quite literal? Freud's notion of symbolism to disguise the real meaning of the dream makes no sense when the point is to warn of life-threatening danger. There is one clue to the reason for fanciful imagery about such serious content: Very few of these dreams are attributed to dozing or napping. They appear to come from deeper sleep; probably most of them are happening during REM.

British researcher Mark Solms found that the areas of the brain that are active in dreaming are ones associated with visual imagery and emotional, metaphoric thinking, while those associated with some fine points of logic are quiet. The hypnagogic state may not be different enough from waking to sense body processes. Once we are deeply enough asleep to do such detection, the caliber of our thinking about what the dreams mean has deteriorated. The mind knows only that it senses burning in a certain area; the demon image is inserted as a visual representation.

Although they have this visual, metaphoric quality, these dreams differ from most in their vividness and repetitiveness. Boss, Sacks, and Stepakoff, as well as Kasatkin's research, mention this repetition—either through the same night or on later nights. Recurring dreams are universally thought to be ones of unusual significance for the dreamer. As we've already seen with Loewi's frog experiment and Beethoven's symphony, when an unconscious part of ourselves has something important to tell us, it tends to repeat itself until the waking mind gets—and remembers—the message.

The "divine" dreams telling a sleeper of illness through a character such as Asclepius may be personifications of our own subliminal sensations. We have many centers of cognition, only a few of which reach consciousness at a given point in time. Some of these subsystems may have special access to sensory input about our body processes and health. People with multiple-personality disorder often have one personality that can sense body processes extremely well. Other personalities are likely to tune them out totally. Just as other aspects of ourselves appear as Einstein when presenting computer solutions, those of ancient Greeks may have masqueraded as Asclepius when dealing with body sensations on the basis of the same type of emotional and visual associations.

Most dreams that solve medical problems address ones specific to the dreamer. But sometimes a physician dreams something of general relevance to medical science—more like the examples in chapters 5 and 6. Canadian physician Frederick Banting was knighted for developing a method of isolating the hormone insulin after seeing the technique in a dream.[18] In *The Dream Game*, Ann Faraday recounts a surgeon's development of a technique for tying off a surgical knot with his left hand while his right is crucially occupied, after dreaming of the maneuver.[19]

Medical examples make up most body dreams, but there is another physical arena to which the Committee contributes: that of the athlete.

Sleep Acrobatics: Sports Enhancement Through Dreams

We fly in our dreams and move through walls. But sometimes we perform novel activities that can be put to good use in the physical world. Just as with any special skill, professionals—in this case athletes—are more likely to have such dreams.

In 1964, golfer Jack Nicklaus had a bad slump, shooting in the high seventies. After suddenly regaining top scores, he reported,

> Wednesday night I had a dream and it was about my golf swing. I was hitting them pretty good in the dream and all at once I realized I wasn't holding the club the way I've actually been holding it lately. I've been having trouble collapsing my right arm taking the club head away from the ball, but I was doing it perfectly in my sleep. So when

I came to the course yesterday morning, I tried it the way I did in my dream and it worked. I shot a sixty-eight yesterday and a sixty-five today.[20]

The 1960 world heavyweight boxing champion Floyd Patterson literally dreamed up new punches many times. He would try these in his next fight. They were always moves that his opponents weren't expecting. Some were added to his permanent repertoire, while others were quickly discarded.

The greatest gymnastic feat of all time also originated in a dream. World-famous acrobat Tito Gaona told *Sports Illustrated*, "I have sometimes dreamed my tricks at night . . . and then tried to master them from the dream . . . I do what I call a double-double . . . it is a double forward somersault with a double full twist at the same time. It has never been done before. No one else does it. It is a trick I dreamed one night."[21]

More recently, women's track superstar Marion Jones has been having a recurring dream that is a source of major inspiration, if vague on technique. Jones describes it as her "Perfect Day" dream: It's a beautiful morning; breakfast is delicious; she's at the track on time. Her start at the gun is flawless and her stride fleet. It's so easy that it feels like a regular race and she can't understand why everyone else is far behind. Jones crosses the finish line and looks back at the clock—she's set a new world record.[22]

The Committee doesn't ignore amateur athletes either. When *Washington Post* writer Don Oldenburg interviewed me about my research for an article on problem-solving in dreams, he ended up telling me of his own experience. "About the time I turned forty," Oldenburg recalled, "I was losing the power of my serve. I'd tried a number of things to try to get it back, and nothing had worked. Then I had a dream—it was like an anatomy illustration. It wasn't me, yet I knew it was conveying the posture I had to take to serve. I could see how the stroke came across the ball from a totally different angle. I woke up and told my wife I had to go to the tennis court before work and try it. I did, and it worked! I've used it ever since." Oldenburg says that he's also come up with story leads occasionally in dreams, but that this sports example is by far the most successful practical dream he's had.

Robert Van de Castle writes in his book *The Dreaming Mind* of a friend who bought an old-fashioned high-wheeled bicycle and spent three months repairing it. During that time he had several joyous dreams of riding it that made him feel he knew how. When the repairs were finished, the dreamer found he could ride it on his very first try. He had learned the balancing skills in his dreams.[23]

Another mundane but important concern was addressed by the Committee when Oliver Sacks was recovering from a leg injury and needed to advance from using two crutches to only one:

> I tried this twice, and both times fell flat on my face. I could not consciously think how to do it. Then I fell asleep, and had a dream in which I reached out my right hand, grabbed the crutch that hung over my head, tucked it under my right arm, and set off with perfect confidence and ease down the corridor. Waking from the dream, I reached out my right hand, grabbed the crutch that hung over the bed, and set off with perfect confidence and ease down the corridor.[24]

Peter and Elizabeth Fenwick recount a similar example in their book *The Hidden Door*. A man who'd lost his leg in an auto accident had grown accustomed to walking on an artificial one for several years, but had lingering difficulties in climbing stairs. One night he dreamed he was ascending a spiral staircase as he had been taught—lifting the good leg up, moving the artificial left foot level with it, and lifting the good leg up again. Someone behind him on the stairs asked why he was climbing this way. The patient told him he'd lost a leg, but the dream character had a better way: when he lifted the artificial foot up, he should lean back so the arch of the foot touched the edge of the upper step, then bring the good foot up to the next step.

Still dreaming, he followed these instructions and found it worked well. The character then told him to turn around, and told him how to descend in a similar manner. "I found this method quite safe," reported the dreamer, "and realized it was still in a dream. . . . The one thing he insisted on, though, is that I do not try it unless I have a good handrail to my left for ascending, or to my right for descending. . . ."

This dreamer did not attempt the suggested movement for months, but the dream stayed with him. "Try as I might, I just could not cast its memory away, so one afternoon I went to try to go up and down stairs as instructed, just to see its effect, and after thirty minutes, found it quite easy to do, so that now traveling on the underground [subway] my leg is no obstacle for fellow travelers."[25]

Athletes have long used waking visualization for rehearsal and improvement. Pitchers imagine snapping off their best curve ball over and over, quarterbacks fantasize hitting the wide receiver in stride, and basketball players practice that perfect dunk in their mind's eye, convinced that the body will follow suit. Many athletes never let themselves picture anything going wrong with their game because they believe the body will do the last thing the brain thought. Much of this lore is exaggerated, but there is some truth to it. More and more coaches and specialized sports psychologists train teams in visualization. Recent research finds that imagining a movement enhances later performance much as physical training does. This covert practice has the advantage of working the less fatigable brain while conserving muscle energy.

I recently collaborated with Dar Tavanaiepour on a study of the effects of visualization on swimmers' performance. Currently a medical student, Dar is also an accomplished swimmer and amateur swim coach. He contributed the technical knowledge on a sport about which I know little. Because of the traditional two-week time-out from practice between the main swim season and the final meets of the year, during which muscles are allowed to recover strength, competitive swimming is an ideal activity in which to examine imagery. On average, swimmers' times improve after this rest, but coaches assume this effect is diminished by the atrophy of skills. Innovative coaches have instituted regular visualized swimming practice during the two-week period to try to prevent this kind of atrophy. Tavanaiepour and I gathered data from the two Pennsylvania college swim teams that used such imagery and the remaining ten that did not. All teams improved in their average times between the regular season and the final meet, but the teams practicing visualized swimming improved almost twice as much!

Tavanaiepour and I hypothesize that nocturnal dreamed practice might be more vivid than waking imagery, and might thus improve skills with innovations rather than just maintain them. So we are doing a second study in which swimmers are encouraged to have lucid dreams in which they practice swimming. For most swimmers, this is harder to achieve than waking visualization. But it has been dramatically effective for those who can learn to do it. The following dreams are from two swimmers who experienced greater improvement after their two-week rest during which the dreams occurred:

> When I started to bounce up and down with both legs, as I usually do before a race to warm up, I noticed it took a little longer than usual to land back on the ground. I didn't think much of it. But I knew I was dreaming when I jumped off the starting blocks and it took a while before I entered the pool. As I was swimming, I began to see myself and the other swimmers next to me from an outside perspective. I could observe my technique and compare it with the other swimmers that had the perfect technique the coach had been talking about. I did not have much control, but finally realized what was wrong with my technique and what the ideal technique that the coach had been talking about looked like.
>
> In the middle of the race I looked over to the swimmer next to me. He was wearing clothing that I thought was odd. After swimming for a while I looked again and the swimmer had transformed into my coach. I could hear the coach encouraging me to swim faster. He said as long as I swam at his pace, I would win the race and achieve

my goal time. I didn't have much control except whenever my coach would speed up I would be able to keep up with him, hoping to beat my best time.[26]

We will examine other research on problem solving and dreams in the final chapter. But first, in Chapter 8, we'll see how other cultures use the dream state.

8

WHEN GANDHI DREAMED OF RESISTANCE: THE COMMITTEE IN NON-WESTERN CULTURES

Mid-nineteenth-century Europeans were fond of citing language as setting man apart from animals and written language as separating "civilized" from "primitive" peoples. Europeans grew critical of America's institution of slavery once they no longer shared in its economic spoils, but they viewed Negroes as inferior. Africa's exclusively oral tradition was invoked to reinforce this prejudice. White audiences never tired of missionaries' stories of natives amazed by the magic of conveying thoughts silently on scraps of pulped wood.

In 1849, Edwin Norris, a British naval officer, returned from antislavery patrol in Liberia and was invited to speak in the oak-paneled Great Hall of London's Royal Geographic Society. He chose to describe the written language of the Vai (sometimes spelled "Vei") tribe—complete with sophisticated script samples. The audience greeted his talk with amazement and incredulity. Common listeners were dubious that Africans could develop a written language on their own. Sophisticated linguists were more baffled because the script was a highly advanced one.

The German-born linguist S. W. Koelle booked passage on a schooner and headed straight for Liberia to confirm the discovery. Landing in the country's port capital, Monrovia, he observed elaborate wooden houses and an affluence that belied stereotypes of Africa. Nearly everyone was writing in Vai, just as Norris had described. Most excitingly, Liberians told Koelle that the alphabet had come into being just fifteen years before, and that the phenomenal literacy rate had been achieved in that time. The distinctive written system had been invented by one Dualu Bukele of Cape Mount.

Koelle hiked fifty miles inland through the humid rain forest with a native guide and translator. The houses dwindled to mud huts. Tropical disease was rampant among the farmers of the rice and cassava fields. But even here, most Vai men and some women were literate—well above the rate for rural Europe or America at that time! When Koelle reached the foothills of Cape Mount, he located Bukele and asked him how he came to invent the marvelous alphabet. Readers will have guessed its origin.

"Fifteen years ago," Bukele told him, "I had a dream in which a tall, venerable-looking white man, in a long coat, appeared to me saying: 'I am sent to you by other white men. . . . I bring you a book.'" The messenger opened the book and showed Bukele signs for every syllable of the Vai language. When Bukele awoke, he recalled only part of what he'd seen, but he wrote down as many of the symbols as he could remember. Later that day, Bukele summoned five young friends to his hut and told them his dream. They helped him make new signs for those he failed to recall. The community elders were so impressed with the ability of the young men to communicate across distances that they established makeshift schools throughout the land to teach everyone the dreamed script.

Unfortunately, Koelle did not record which signs were directly from the dream, but he makes clear that the dream contained the idea of representing Vai in writing, the choice of the syllable as a unit, and some of the individual symbols. Later anthropologists and linguists have concluded that Koelle's account from Bukele is accurate. It matches those of subsequent informants except that some described a few preexisting pictographs of one-syllable words that were incorporated into the alphabet. Again, we can't know whether these were among the dreamed or waking contributions.

Although he was excited by the Vai script, Koelle brought with him some of his contemporaries' prejudices. In studying spoken Vai, he explained to natives the concept of similes, and asked if their culture used these. They offered, *"Poro-mo beiro musu gbandawau,"* meaning "The European is like an unmarried woman"— that is, he changes his liaisons as often as he pleases. Koelle quoted this humorlessly as evidence that the African figurative language was simplistic. He doesn't appear to have considered that the natives chose the line for its content rather than its style.[1]

Modern linguists give the Vai language high marks, noting the simple yet elegant correspondence of the written and spoken forms. Most syllabic alphabets are cumbersome, but Vai lends itself well to this format because it contains only consonant-vowel-consonant sounds. In the 1970s, psycholinguists Sylvia Scribner and Michael Cole visited Liberia and found Vai writers able to express themselves more accurately than those fluent in many other languages. They reported that Vai literacy has survived despite the Liberian government's policy, since assuming control of the schools, of teaching only English. Scribner and Cole attributed the ease of home learning to the efficiency of the dreamed alphabet.[2]

We have drawn the dream creations in previous chapters mostly from Western culture, where people are not taught to listen to their dreams. Many non-Western societies, including those in much of Africa, make extensive use of dreaming. For them, problem solving in dreams is an explicit expectation, not a fluke. Bukele didn't need to justify his dream as a legitimate source of inspiration for waking behavior.

Recall another African example discussed in the music chapter—how Joseph Shabalala receives much of his music in dreams. Explaining his decision to turn the nocturnal music into reality, Shabalala says, "My father was an herbalist and my mother was a diviner. Those are the people who are working with spirits all the time. They depend on and trust their dreams."[3]

The Tukulor tradition of African weaving is also said to have originated in a dream. The legendary ancestor, Beram, dreamed one night of a huge frame device. He didn't know what the device was, but later dreams told Beram it was a loom, and showed him how to weave on it. Whatever the truth of this folklore, modern Tukulor weavers do get all of their inspirations in dreams—from seeing new patterns and color combinations to finding materials for cloth and redesigning the looms.[4]

DREAMS IN INDIA

India is another modern society that places great faith in dreams. In Chapter 5 I discussed how the Indian genius Ramanujan reported that the goddess Namagiri delivered his mathematical formulas in dreams. He was raised with the tradition of listening to dreams. While pregnant with him, his mother dreamed that the goddess would one day speak through her son. When Ramanujan was invited to England, his parents visited the temple of the goddess to incubate a dream. Should they make an exception to religious injunctions against foreign travel? The goddess approved the plan in a dream, and off went their son to attain fame as a mathematician.[5]

The Indian psychologist Anjali Hazarika, who coaches oil executives and engineers, emphasizes that her techniques are drawn from Western dreamwork, predominantly American. However, Hazarika told me her task is easier in presenting dreamwork to Indian businessmen than it would be in the country where the techniques originated. Her listeners have been raised with the religious and folk tradition of deities bringing guidance dreams. They've also heard that the most important political event in modern India was modeled after a dream.

Mahatma Gandhi first worked in a South African law firm and led nonviolent protests against racial discrimination there. In 1915 he returned to British-ruled India and supported the Allies during the First World War by raising and leading an ambulance corps. After cooperating in the war effort, India expected to receive Dominion status. Instead, in 1919 the Rowlatt Acts were passed by the Indian national legislature. These acts aimed to curtail civil liberties of Indians in the name of preventing terrorist violence. The entire country viewed the legislation as a grievous insult, but they were a minority in their own legislature. Gandhi made the only appearance of his life in the legislative chamber to argue against the Rowlatt Acts—to no avail. He felt at a loss about what to do if they passed into law. But the morning after reading of their final passage, Gandhi had his plan of action.

"The idea came to me last night in a dream that we should call upon the country to observe a general *hartal* [hunger strike]," Gandhi wrote. "Ours is a sacred fight, and it seems to me to be in the fitness of things that it should be commenced with an act of self-purification. Let all the people of India, therefore, suspend their business on that day and observe the day as one of fasting and prayer." Gandhi and his allies drafted a call for a *hartal* on April 6 of that year. Newspapers throughout India published the plea. "The whole of India from one end to the other, towns as well as villages, observed a complete *hartal* on that day," he recounted in his autobiography. "It was a most wonderful spectacle." Thus began the nonviolent campaign against British rule, which featured many hunger strikes and culminated in the independence of India nearly three decades later.[6] It is unlikely that a Western leader would have taken a dream suggestion this literally.

Physicist Anita Goel, whose parents emigrated from India, was born and has studied in the United States. This gives her an excellent perspective on the differences between the two cultures. Goel shared with me one of the problem-solving dreams she'd had, and how she felt it was influenced by her Indian heritage:

> One evening when I was an undergraduate at Stanford, I'd been working late in lab and got home during the wee hours. The next morning I had a statistical mechanics exam. Because I'd been so focused on meeting some research deadlines, I hadn't begun to prepare for this exam. I slept 2 to 3 hours that night and then did my usual morning meditation. Around 4:30 A.M., I started

hitting the books for the exam. I was feeling slightly over-whelmed, to say the least. I thought to myself that per-haps only a miracle would allow me to learn all this in the few hours remaining before the exam. I skimmed what-ever I could of the material within two hours and sank into a short catnap around the crack of dawn.

All of a sudden in a half-asleep state, I felt like I was moving and I came upon some sort of screen and projec-tor. I started feeling thoughts about Bose-Einstein con-densation. Then they sped up so fast that I could no longer keep up with their content and I started visualiz-ing equations condensing on the screen and had the sense of deriving things. The whole thing must have lasted for only a couple of minutes. I felt a bit numb and absent-minded, as if my brain had grasped some sort of infor-mation or understanding that I was not yet consciously aware of. I got up and looked at the books some more, and went to take my exam.

I started taking the test. I felt very relaxed and com-pleted the test in about twenty minutes. As I looked around, I was surprised to see folks rushing to finish at the end of the fifty-minute period. Later that evening, after I got some more sleep, I started thinking that per-haps I had left half the exam blank.

At the next class meeting, the professor put a his-togram on the board with the exam results. He was very disappointed: the average was about a 12. The highest looked like a 17. He said something about one score being so off the scale that he didn't even want to put it up. I got my test back and saw that it had a 2 and a 9 on it. As he was chastising the whole class, I was taking all this in, thinking that, yup, I really didn't study the way I should have.

After class, as I was leaving, he stopped me and said he would like to have a little chat with me. "How did you do this?!" I was still thinking myself that he meant, "how could you do so badly?"

I told him rather apologetically that I didn't know, but I was sure that I would do better next time. So I was surprised when he started praising me. It suddenly dawned on me that my score was a 29—the one off-scale score he didn't put up on the histogram!

Goel told me the equations in the dream went too fast to be sure but she thinks they were similar to the ones she was dealing with on the exam—and certainly on the same topic. "It literally felt like knowledge and insight into these problems had rapidly poured into my brain in a very subtle way," she says of the dream. "The primary mode was visual. I felt rapid thoughts as I saw them condense into visual equations."

Goel has often dreamed of ideas that she later executed. She credits much of this to her meditative and analytical practices. Her problem-solving dreams are often more vivid than her other dreams. She is lucid in them. "With these kinds of dreams I can control what's happening—I know it's a dream," she says. "I often say 'Okay, here it goes,' and sometimes I try to censor them saying, 'let's not let this strange thing happen right now.' But that time I did."

Without her Eastern roots, Goel doubts she would have heeded such dreams and could have easily suppressed them. "Here I feel a bit funny that I should even be talking to you about these things," she told me.

This may be more true of Western science than of other disciplines. Composer Sharish Korde, whose dreamed compositions were discussed in Chapter 4, is also an American of Indian heritage. "I think the way I dream of music is colored by my Hindu upbringing," Korde told me. "I'll sometimes dream of Krishna—the god is also a flute player—bringing music. But once I've dreamed a piece, I think either an Eastern or a Western composer would certainly write it down." The artists I interviewed were uniformly eager to recount inspirations from dreams. Some scientists, mathematicians, and businesspeople hesitated to reveal dreams as the source of their insights—so cross-cultural differences may be greater in these realms. Art has always been the subdivision of Western culture that most values unconscious, nonlinear thought.

DREAMS AND ISLAM

Yet another region where dreams have an honored tradition of problem solving is the Middle East—especially the Islamic world. Again, the respect stems partly from the belief in dreams as divine messages.

Muhammad received his notice that he was the greatest of all prophets through an epic dream in which he was guided by the archangel Gabriel across the seven celestial spheres. He conferred with Abraham and Jesus along the way, then returned to earth to write of the experience as his sixty-five-page *Nocturnal Journey*. Later, Muhammad also experienced much of the Koran in his dreams.

Each morning, Muhammad and his disciples would share and interpret dreams. He ordered the practice of *adhan*—the daily call to prayer from the minarets, and a central ritual of Islam to this day—after one of his followers dreamed of it.[7] The split of Islam into conflicting Sunni and Shi'ite factions springs partly from a dream of Muhammad, which the Sunnis used to justify their rights as his successors, while the Shi'ites trace theirs to a biological lineage from his son.[8]

The Islamic world continues to take dream divination very seriously in this century. Autobiographies of rulers often contain extensive dream diaries and accounts of decisions ostensibly based on dreams. One example occurred when the Shah of Iran was deciding whether to seek a loan from Russia. "He dreamed that a famous theological figure dressed in primitive Muslim garb approached the Shah and threw at his feet a sack containing gold and silver. The fairly obvious interpretation of this dream was that the Shah shouldn't make any new loans with unbelievers but should trust that his subjects and fellow servants of the faith would restore his finances."[9]

Iraq has a long-standing dispute with Kuwait over oil fields that Iraq claims were originally Iraqi land. In August of 1990, Saddam Hussein pressed this claim by invading Kuwait. The Gulf War—which he would have won easily within days, if not for Western military intervention—occurred, Hussein claimed, because he had a dream in which he was told to take back the oil fields. In cultures that prize dreams as a source of inspiration, the potential for distortion lies in the opposite direction from ours. Unlike Goel, who hesitates to tell westerners the source of her mathematical proofs, the Shah and Hussein may gain credibility for their ideas if they claim they originated in dreams. When such dreams are expected, however, it is also likely more of them genuinely occur. Dreams prove quite malleable to beliefs and suggestion.

I flew to Kuwait shortly after the Gulf War to train Kuwaiti psychologists in treating post-traumatic stress disorder. Most dream discussions focused on the recurring traumatic nightmares many Kuwaitis experienced. Because of the Muslim belief in dreams as messages for action, there was little of the assumption—a given in Western traditions—that dreams arise from the dreamer's past. Dreams of the Iraqis invading again were even more anxiety-provoking for Kuwaitis than they would be in other cultures.[10] My students, who had some respect for Western psychology, welcomed the information that trauma victims elsewhere have recurring dreams about those horrors without seeing them repeated. Westernized Kuwaitis were visibly relieved just to hear this. More-traditional Muslims dismissed this interpretation.

There was a positive side to the emphasis on dreams foretelling the future. During the occupation, some Kuwaitis had dreamed of the Iraqis leaving. Those dreams were a source of great inspiration, and made the occupation bearable. In a Western country, dreamers would probably have dismissed the visions as "wish fulfillment." Kuwaiti psychologist Badria al Badaii told me of dreaming of the invaders being driven out. She saw the soldiers occupying the house across the way rising from a half-eaten meal and running away. She heard the voice of Allah telling her she would need to be strong for others until this happened. Later, she did witness soldiers departing in exactly this manner. Other Kuwaitis described deciding whether to remain in the city during the occupation or to leave for Saudi Arabia, based on what they had seen in their dreams.

The most astonishing Kuwaiti dream story I heard was that the discovery of the disputed oil fields was credited to a dream—of a westerner, but one long steeped in the tradition of the Muslim desert. Lieutenant Colonel H. Dickson was the British military commander in charge of the Bedouin desert area that is now Kuwait. British engineers were drilling for oil there. One afternoon Dickson made camp early because a dust storm was approaching. He set up his tent and retreated inside. The storm blew a large hole at the foot of a nearby palm tree. That night Dickson dreamed that he went to the hole—now deeper than in real life—and, peering down, beheld an ancient sarcophagus. Its lid opened and a beautiful young girl reached out of it, imploring him, "Don't let them bury me!" Dickson was struck by the vivid dream—and also very involved with the search for oil in the area. After talking to a Bedouin woman who reinforced his feeling that the dream was a command to action, he got the drilling operations moved to the spot underneath the tree. The drill sank into the richest oil field in the history of the world.

Kuwaitis tell this story as a divine or psychic event, but it was dreamed by a man savvy about the oil industry and desert geography. As with other contributions of the Committee, Dickson's unconscious may have been processing knowledge he already possessed. The dream-honoring culture in which he lived, however, certainly helped give the message a hearing.

NATIVE AMERICAN DREAMS

Many indigenous societies in the western hemisphere—north and south—see dreams as a source of creativity and guidance. Several years ago, *Arizona Highways* magazine interviewed a series of prominent Native American artists from various tribes. The interviewer was impressed that when he asked where their ideas came from, they almost always replied, "I had this dream. . . ." Sometimes the dream determined simply the content of the piece. White Buffalo sculpted a large silver bust after he dreamed of a man with silver hair and a silver face. Occasionally a dream initiated a career in art. Jeweler Jesse Monongye began making jewelry after dreaming his deceased mother gave him files and stone-cutting tools and told him that if he took these he would become a famous artist. He won a major award for his very first piece of inlaid jewelry inspired by that dream.[11]

Not all Native American tribes put equal emphasis on dreams. The Xanvante, Cree, Ojibwa, and Iroquois are among the most dream-oriented. In Africa, Joseph Shabalala chose to sing his dream songs—but the Xanvante Indians of Central Brazil make this a sacred duty. Xanvante male initiation rites include receiving dream songs from ancestral spirits. The spirits sing and dance the young man's song in a dream. When the initiate awakens, he knows to sing the song softly to himself so as to fix it in his memory. This is not unlike Western advice on how to remember dreams. Later in the day, the young man teaches his peers the song, and he is known by it from then on.[12]

The Cree of Quebec also honor spirits who appear in dreams. Their spirits, however, are animal guides who help with the never-ending task of hunting. "Everything a man uses in hunting, he has to dream first," insist the Cree. Clothing, weapons, and hunting chants all appear in dreams.[13]

The Ojibwa routinely make most of their art, clothing, and housing based on dreams. They are also given their names and professions this way. The Iroquois routinely bring dreams of events and devices to community gatherings. The tribe helps them convert these into waking reality.

EFFECTS OF DREAM EMPHASIS

What types of ideas does the Committee deliver in cultures that listen this closely? Are they different from those the occasionally attentive westerner receives, or simply more frequent?

Anthropologist Michele Stephens summarizes the effects of dream-emphasizing cultures across Melanesia: "Inventions and innovations of all kinds are revealed in dreams to specialists, and to ordinary men and women."[14] Most of her examples are visual. Ceremonial masks are the objects most often based on dreams, but inventions of all kinds occur. The pattern is similar among the Australian Aborigines, who honor what they call *Dreamtime*—a concept that includes mythic events and waking trance states as well as nighttime dreaming. The Aborigines' best-known dream products are their distinctive dot-paintings on bark, but many other inventions and decisions come to them in dreams. Patterns of problem-solving dreams in these cultures are similar to those found in the West—albeit intensified. Creative dreams come to the most prepared, and visual arts still dominate the Committee's emphasis.

Many popular dream books romanticize indigenous cultures as empowering their members to use dreams. They contrast this with Western cultures, which designate psychotherapists as the dream experts. Many tribal dream traditions, however, honor the dreams of only a few people. The shaman alone may have dreams considered "true," or he may be needed to interpret the dreams of others. The use of the male pronoun here is not incidental—many of these cultures value the dreams of men more than those of women.

The Siberian shaman receives his calling in a dream, and learns most of his healing techniques the same way. He, rather than the patient, would be expected to have a diagnostic dream about the state of the ill person's body. Such cultures do not put most people in touch with the Committee. Even the chosen few who have such dreams view them as coming from outside themselves rather than as enhancing their own talents.

In Kate Horsley's novel *Crazy Woman*, about eighteenth-century Navajos, her fictional villain is the tribe's medicine man. He pretends to have a dream calling him to heal. This is the only role by which one clearly destined to be a poor hunter can enjoy great prestige within his tribe. The first alleged dream leads to a need to fake many others, as he goes about trying to cure the sick. He lives in fear of being discovered as an imposter. Horsley's account is fiction, but it's easy to imagine such a thing occurring in such cultures—in much the same way a Middle Eastern leader might be tempted to report self-serving political advice from dreams.

Still, anthropologists believe most of these stories are real. The training the shaman undertakes does produce dreams about healing consistently on demand, just as intensive practice for dream lucidity produces more awareness within dreams. Cultures that emphasize creative dreams for everyone do indeed have more of them. Equally important, those cultures are more likely to analyze dreams that are more cryptic in nature to mine their potential yield.

The one dream-enhancement technique that has been researched in our culture is dream incubation. The next chapter examines what studies show about its effectiveness and what we may be able to do with our own dreams.

9

What Word Starts and Ends With "He"? Sleep on a Brainteaser and Wake Up with a Headache

Psychiatrist Morton Schatzman gave a fellow physician an expanded version of the title brainteaser—one that suggested it had two solutions. The young doctor "slept on it" and dreamed the following:

> I'm cutting flowers in my garden. I get an intense pain in my chest and fall over. Juliet, the woman I live with in real life, comes out of the house laughing. Her laugh is not her usual one, but is a squeaky "hee . . . hee . . . hee . . . hee." Her laughter puzzles and hurts me, because I want her sympathy. She calls an ambulance, and I'm taken to the hospital. I tell the ambulance driver to hurry, as the pain is severe. I ask him why it's taking so long. He says the road is blocked; a brain has fallen out onto the road and must be removed before traffic can proceed. We arrive

and I'm wheeled through the front door of the hospital. Many people are gathered there, all laughing in the same way that Juliet was. I try to cover my ears, but I can't bring my fingers together to keep the sounds out. I'm in the ward. A doctor says, "I know what's wrong with you."

"Then take the pain away," I reply.

"I can, but I won't. You must tell me what is wrong with you, and then you'll be better and can go home."

"I've had a coronary," I answer.

"Jargon isn't good enough."

"I'm a doctor and I'm being precise and technical," I reply.

"I've been forbidden to discharge you until you tell me in plain language what your problem is." All this time, behind his hand he's been laughing with a high-pitched "hee . . . hee . . . hee."

I get very angry. "You're infuriating!" I say. "Why do you keep laughing? I could have my pain forever. You could call it anything, even heartache." He stops laughing.

"You can go home," he says.

I still feel pain, but now I don't know where it is. "I'm not quite better," I tell him.

"You must see another doctor, a word specialist."

I leave the hospital, and Morton Schatzman appears. "I hear you're not quite well," Morton says. "I told you that there were two things wrong with you."

"I just want to go to sleep and not think about it."

"You can go to sleep any time you want," he replies, "but you must learn to juggle words and pains."

"Riddles give me headaches," I tell him. My pain goes away completely and I feel well.[1]

The dreamer awoke knowing the answers to the problem: HEartacHE and HEadacHE. At what point in his dream did you see each solution appear?

Formal research on problem solving tells us how often and in what manner the Committee's solutions arrive. Studies have been going on for over a century. In 1892, Charles Child asked 186 college students whether they'd ever solved a problem in a dream. One-third of the students said they had. Examples included a chess game played in a dream, an algebra problem solved, a bookkeeping error detected, and a passage from Virgil deftly translated.[2]

In 1972, William Dement used brainteasers to study the phenomena. He asked five hundred college students to solve several of them over three consecutive nights. Dement taught them a simpler version of the dream incubation techniques we explored in Chapter 7—asking them only to study the problem for fifteen minutes before sleep, to keep paper by the bed, and to record their dreams. Of 1,148 attempts at solving problems (not every student followed through each night), eighty-seven resulted in dreams that the experimenters judged to address a problem. Seven dreams solved one of them. Other accounts contained correct solutions, but the dreamer reported reaching it before falling asleep, so the dream merely echoed that.

Dement's first problem was "The letters O, T, T, F, F . . . form the beginnings of an infinite sequence. Find a simple rule for determining any or all successive letters. According to your rule, what would be the next two letters of the sequence?" One subject dreamed this answer:

I was walking down the hall of an art gallery. I began to count the paintings—one, two, three, four, five. But as I came to the sixth and seventh, the paintings had been ripped from their frames! I stared at the empty frames with a peculiar feeling that some mystery was about to be solved. Suddenly I realized that the sixth and seventh spaces were the solution to the problem. [The sequence is the first letter of each number, so the next two would be "S, S" for six and seven.][3]

A few students had dreams that hinted at the solution without the waking mind catching on—a phenomenon to which we'll return later in the chapter. Dement noted that all dreams providing solutions occurred on the first of the three nights in which students incubated dreams. He speculated that the novelty of brainteasers and dream incubation dissipated quickly and the subjects were not as engaged on subsequent nights.

SOLVING PERSONALLY MEANINGFUL PROBLEMS IN DREAMS

For my own research in 1993, I let students incubate problems of their own choosing so they would have more personal meaning.[4] This parallels spontaneous uses of problem solving more closely than do brainteasers. I specified only that the problem must matter to them, and that it must have a recognizable solution. I gave the longer version of dream incubation outlined in Chapter 7. I also shared with my subjects the results of Dement's research and several of the historic examples of dream creativity and problem solving, so my students had a positive model of the potential of dreamwork.

Each night for a week, students incubated a dream on their problem. They recorded their dreams and noted ones they thought addressed the problem or contained a satisfactory solution. Two independent judges rated whether the dreams merely focused on the problems or actually solved them.

My subjects chose a range of issues from academic, medical, and personal categories. These appeared easier than Dement's brainteasers. Whether because of this ease, or owing to the relevance to my students' lives, two-thirds had dreams they felt addressed their problem. One-third dreamed solutions. Judges rated only slightly fewer dreams as addressing or solving problems. Many problems that were solved concerned major life decisions. The following example was rated as solved by both the dreamer and the judges:

> PROBLEM: I have applied to two clinical psychology programs and two in industrial psychology because I just can't decide which field I want to go into.
>
> DREAM: A map of the United States. I'm in a plane flying over this map. The pilot says we're having engine trouble and need to land. We look for a safe place on the map indicated by a light. I ask about Massachusetts, which we're right over, but he says that all of Massachusetts is very dangerous. The lights seemed to be farther west.
>
> SOLUTION: I woke up and realized that my two clinical schools are both in Massachusetts, where I've spent my whole life and where my parents live. Both industrial

programs are far away, Texas and California. This is because originally I was looking to stay close to home and there were no good industrial programs nearby. I realized that there is a lot wrong with staying at home and, funny as it sounds, getting away is probably more important than which kind of program I go into.

Some dreams were literal depictions of problems and solutions. Here are three examples: A young man had been asked to make a tuition deposit by one medical school before he'd heard from his preferred ones; he dreamed of receiving rejections from the others. A woman who'd been having trouble with her menstrual cycle dreamed of a doctor telling her the problem was her extreme diet and exercise regime. A student trying to remember whether she'd taken a medication dreamed of having swallowed it.

Other problems appeared in the dreams as metaphors:

PROBLEM: I'm trying to decide whether to be on the softball team again this spring. I love it, but practice does take time away from my studies. I could just go watch the games this year and still see my friends from the team.

DREAM: I'm camping in an open place in a tent that doesn't come all the way to the ground. People are all around, staring at me. I feel very uncomfortable and exposed.

SOLUTION: The dream reminded me of the phrase "a watcher rather than a doer," which has very negative connotations for me. I don't think I'd be happy with just going to the games.

Judges didn't rate this dream as solving the problem; they favored those with a literal depiction. The one instance in which judges thought a problem was solved and the dreamer didn't was when a dream contained a specific answer to a dichotomous problem, but the subject still felt ambivalent. Judges—as instructed—looked for "*a* solution," while dreamers demanded the *correct* solution.

Dichotomous choices between two preconceived answers have a better chance of a dream solution, but allow less novelty. Some did offer original solutions, like the dream that reframed geographically the choice between two types of graduate programs. Awake, the dreamer hadn't considered that the West promised a necessary change—but the dream pronounced this as primary. The answer was certainly within the range of the subject's waking reasoning. As with the dreams of novelists or inventors, it served to "unstick" a certain train of thought.

Other dichotomous problems were answered simply by favoring one choice over another. This afforded several dreamers a sense of resolution. Other times it did not; as we've said, this is when the dreamers didn't rate the problem as solved. Dreams could involve either side of ambivalent issues. One student debated whether to marry her boyfriend, who was becoming a career army officer. Was she willing to move around the country as a military wife? After incubating the dilemma, she dreamed of their wedding at the country club where she worked—a job she loved. She wore a beautiful gown, and her groom looked handsome in his tux. In this festive scene she felt ecstatic, and she thought of this as a positive answer until:

> Several nights after I had stopped incubating the problem, I again dreamed we were about to get married. I was

begging the people that were with me not to make me do it. I kept saying, "Please don't make me do it! I don't want to marry him! *Please!*" I remember feeling very frightened and very alone. I felt like if I married him, my life would end.

The first dream sets the happy wedding in the current job she'd have to leave, but otherwise the two dreams seem diametrically opposed. After the second, the dreamer was less inclined to take either as an edict—postponing the decision when last I heard. Unlike the issue of whether one took a pill or not, the Committee sent no absolute right answer to the marriage conundrum, although the two problems are framed in the same yes/no format.

Some of my students did choose to try to dream solutions to open-ended problems without preconceived alternatives. These were slightly less likely to be solved than the dichotomous choices, but they offered more chances for novel answers:

PROBLEM: I recently moved from one apartment to a smaller one. Every time I tried to arrange my bedroom furniture in the new room, it looked crowded. I've been trying to decide if there's a better way, or if I will have to get rid of something.

DREAM: I come home and all the boxes are unpacked and pictures hung. Everything looks real nice. The bedroom chest of drawers is in the living room up against the wall like a sideboard and it blends right in there. I'm puzzled because I don't remember doing this. I can't figure out if I moved the chest and unpacked or someone else has, but I like it.

SOLUTION: The chest actually fit there real well when I tried it, so I left it there.

The Committee has no supernatural decorating skills, but nudges the student out of the mindset that bedroom furniture must go in the bedroom.

We've been referring to them as "solving problems," but these examples actually seem to present the dream ego with a solution already arrived at. One doesn't see the dreamer struggling with the problem except in a few of the dreams judged to be addressing but not solving it. Sometimes the dream ego gets the point only after awakening, as with the clinical versus industrial graduate-school map. But some other agency in the dream—in that case the pilot—seems to have prepared the solution in advance. In the furniture-arranging example, the dream ego arrives home to find the solution already in place. In Dement's hallway of paintings for the "O, T, T, F, F . . ." problem, the dreamer is counting near the start and then the empty frames are in the sixth and seventh spots—even though the student consciously "gets it" only when he awakens.

This is also true in the "he-he" dream. The first "hee-hee-hee" might merely announce that the problem is the topic—although some dictionaries give "he-he" as a word for laughter or amusement, making it a third solution to the problem. Very soon the main solutions, "heartache" and "headache," are hinted at in successive order by chest pain and a brain falling into the street. Next the dream badgers the dream ego for the words "in plain English." Finally the dream ego says each aloud.

Most subjects in these experiments didn't clearly see the solution until they woke. The dreams presented the Committee's suggestions, but the dream ego didn't process them. In fact, subjects rarely cared about the problem until they woke. In the "he-he" example, the Committee had to cast the issue as chest pain to get the dreamer's attention—much as the dreaming Elias Howe cared about his sewing machine only because savages were going to kill him if he didn't get it to work. This may be why so many creative and problem-solving dreams are nightmares. Our dream ego is just not concerned with the original problem—but some other part of us is. It grabs our attention with any means at its disposal.

In the work of the "he-he" dream's "word specialist," Morton Schatzman, an American psychiatrist who has spent his career in London, there are more examples that cast light on the process of dreaming a solution.

TEASERS FOR THE BRAINS OF THOUSANDS

Schatzman used a less formal version of Dement's experimental paradigm, giving brainteasers to thousands of people in England via newspapers, magazines, and radio appearances. He had no way of knowing either the total number who incubated dreams or the percentage who solved the problems. Deviations from instructions were probably more frequent than for other experiments. However, Schatzman received dozens of examples that contain rich detail illuminating how the process may work.

One of his puzzles asked, What is distinctive about the sentence 'Show this bold Prussian that praises slaughter, slaughter brings rout.' The solution is that dropping the first letter of each word produces "How his old Russian hat raises laughter, laughter rings out." One respondent dreamed that she handed the paper containing the problem to a woman who *laughed* and told her "the Prussians are coming." Other people then *laugh* and suggest she would be more comfortable if she removed her head. When the dreamer can't do this, one man exclaims, "Too many letters," her head floats off, and she awakens.

The dream characters immediately acted out the phrase "laughter rings out," then used "Prussians" in a sentence usually associated with "Russians." Removing the head looks like a metaphoric visual version of the suggestion that becomes more direct when the man says, "Too many letters."

Another woman contacted Schatzman after seeing an article in the *London Sunday Times* that contained that same puzzle and also "Which of the following verbs does not belong in this group: *bring, catch, draw, fight, seek, teach*, and *think?*" She wrote:

> In my dream I'm watching Michael Caine in one of his spy roles, possibly *The Ipcress File*. He's in the Centre, or whatever spy headquarters is called.
>
> He walks up to a door marked COMPUTER ROOM and opens it; behind the door is a heavy wire-mesh screen. He passes a folded copy of the *Sunday Times* to someone behind the screen.
>
> From the computer room come sounds of whirring tapes, clickings and other computer-type noises. I see that through a slot in the grille is being pushed a colored comic postcard with a caption at the bottom. Michael Caine takes it, looks at it, chuckles briefly, and hands it to me.
>
> The postcard comes to life, and I'm sitting in an audience watching a stage show. On the stage, a comic

Elizabethan figure in doublet and hose, wearing a hat with an enormous feather, is kneeling with his head in a guillotine. He looks apprehensively at the audience and rolls his eyes. The audience rocks with laughter, and the comic figure struggles to his feet, comes to the front of the stage, and says, "Sh-sh-sh! Laughter is a capital offense!" More riotous laughter from the audience. The comic figure doffs his hat with a flourish and bows extravagantly. For some reason I feel very grateful to Michael Caine, and turn to thank him. He says nothing, but points over his shoulder to indicate that he must dash, and with a friendly wave walks off.

The dreamer woke up, examined the first problem, realized its solution involved "lopping off" letters, and began to doze again:

> In my rather sleepy state I wondered what had happened to the answer to the other problem which I felt I should know.
>
> Before actually falling asleep again, I saw Michael Caine looking rather irritable and repeating the pointing gesture over his shoulder. I realized that he was performing a mime and that, just as in the TV show *Give Us a Clue*, pointing over his shoulder indicated past tense. Again I switched on my bedside light and looked at the problem. I saw that the only one of the verbs whose past tense doesn't end in *-ght* was *draw*.[5]

Much as with the first woman's dream, the *Sunday Times* under the arm is the announcement that this dream concerns the problem. The acting out, as in charades, is completely literal. Riotous laughter from the audience "ringing out" is a direct enactment of the hidden sentence. The hints are visual: *hat* is a key word in the answer, but taking it off is also like beheading the words. The guillotine is a more obvious version of this. The only phrase spoken is that "laughter [another key word in the solution] is a capital offense"—capitals often being first letters. This also suggests the relation between *slaughter* and *laughter*.

What are we watching here? Schatzman says it may be that "some component of the dream, already in possession of the answer, was playing hide-and-seek with the dreamer." And later: "Perhaps the agency of the mind from where the contents of a dream emanate does not or cannot communicate its 'messages' in ordinary language." I favor the latter explanation. Theorists since Freud have viewed dreams as intentionally cryptic, but what we see here looks like a progressive struggle. The dream ego is beckoned by an intelligence for whom visual images flow and words are difficult. It resembles the antics of "split brain" patients who have had their left and right hemispheres separated surgically. When their language-weak right brain spots something, it mimes and gestures to try to call it to the attention of the left brain.

The Committee struggles more or less before different dreamers "get it" for different problems. Another of Schatzman's brainteasers was this: "What is remarkable about the following sentence: 'I am not very happy acting pleased whenever prominent scientists overmagnify intellectual enlightenment.'" One reader dreamed:

I am giving a lecture to a number of scientists about hypnosis. They are seated at round tables scattered about a large hall. Nobody is listening to me. This makes me very angry and I shout, *"I am not very happy."* The scientists seated at the tables nearest me look up. I wake up.

It suddenly struck me that the scientists who had responded to me were seated at five separate tables with one scientist at the table nearest to me, two at another table, three at a third table, and so on up to five. I began to feel that numbers were important in this problem, and I counted the number of words in the sentence. As I did so, I realized that it was the number of letters in each word that was important. I counted the letters and arrived at the sequence. 1, 2, 3, . . . 13.

Another reader dreamed of a Count—a nobleman—dealing with the sentence, which finally led the dreamer to *count* the letters in the word. A teletype operator studying the same problem received the most literal answer in his dream:

I am at work and my supervisor tells me to test a particular telegraph line which has been giving trouble. I begin to type on the teleprinter, "The quick brown fox jumps over the lazy dog"—a standard test because it includes every letter of the alphabet. My supervisor tells me to stop doing that and instead to type "123456789."[6]

Among these dream solutions we see visual representation—tables arranged with the right number of people—and a pun on the key word *count*—both the stock-in-trade of the Committee. The most direct answer comes to someone who deals with words and their component letters all day. This dovetails with what we observed in earlier chapters, which described how people who worked with either language or numbers had an abundance of linguistic or numerical images in their problem-solving dreams.

What else may account for differences in the dreams' directness? In other chapters we saw that depth of sleep was a major factor. Schatzman asked subjects when their dreams occurred. Most said they woke from them at their usual morning hour. They did not describe being "half awake." The woman with the two charade dreams was a rare exception. Nor did Schatzman's subjects say the solutions woke them up as many spontaneous instances do. Indeed, as we've seen, it was often well after awakening that they realized they had the answer. It may be that brainteasers don't matter enough for people to "lose sleep over," while more personal problems do.

Consistent with more personal problems, however, many experimental puzzles of a verbal or abstract nature provoked dream solutions represented by a visual image. This was true of Schatzman's examples—scientists at tables, charades acted out— and also in my research. The graduate applicant examined a map showing lights far from home. The softball player saw people peeking under his tent. My student's choice of how to arrange furniture demanded a visual-spatial solution by its very nature. When Schatzman gave a brainteaser that was geometric rather than linguistic, dreamers replied in unprecedented numbers.

"Using six line segments of equal length," Schatzman specified, "can you construct four equilateral triangles, such that the sides of the triangles are the same length as the line segments?"

There is no solution in two dimensions—the initial approach that most people try—but a *three-dimensional* tetrahedron consists of four equilateral triangles bordered by six such line segments.

One reader dreamed she was at the fence of her old primary school when suddenly six rails came together to form a wigwam. The scene changed and the school became her present college. Her chemistry teacher appeared and said "One hundred nine degrees and twenty-eight minutes." Awake, she realized this was the angle between bonds in the methane molecule—a regular tetrahedron. Later yet, she saw that the wigwam also provided the solution.

Another woman dreamed of asking a scientist for the answer. He leaped in the air, encouraging her to do so. Awake, this made her think to "take the triangles up off the surface."

Other dream images about the problem included (1) stereographic drawings—as the dreamer wrote this dream down, he realized three dimensions was the clue; (2) an odd wheel on a bicycle, with the hub outside the plane of the rim—as soon as she visualized it awake, "it collapsed, the rim contracting and pulling three spokes out at an extreme angle to form a tetrahedron"; and (3) a triangle of metal tent poles lying on the ground while a tripod of poles spun above it, forming various three-dimensional shapes.

In one dream, the dreamer actually heard a voice:

> I am constructing two equilateral triangles by laying six matches flat on a mirror, so that by looking sideways I can see four triangles. At this point a voice says, "That's cheating." After a pause the voice says, "Try three-dimensional." At that point the solution became immediately obvious.[7]

Schatzman cited this as an example in which the problem isn't solved as the dream begins. He suggests that we see the dreaming mind struggling with it—the dreamer constructing triangles on a mirror being the first step, even though he rejects this as "cheating" before the voice offers the better suggestion. My impression is that this dream may belong with the majority in which the solution is implicit from the start of the dream. I think we're watching the usual routine of visual hints—like the mirror—building toward more obvious verbal statements. It depends on what you're attending to—the dream ego is struggling with the problem at the start, but it's not clear the voice doesn't have it all along. A dream that contains a solution can incorporate other ideas from parts of the dreamer that haven't "gotten it." The dreaming mind is not one consistent whole, as is so obvious from the would-be army wife's contradictory series of wedding dreams.

The phenomenon of dreams still dropping hints long after the problem is solved is clearest when the dreamer *never* gets it—but the solution is obvious to others. Several years ago, I was at a dream conference attended by Morton Schatzman and Nancy Parsifal— the woman whose nightmare about anesthesia prompted her to seek natural childbirth. Both were friends of mine, but they'd just met each other. Parsifal heard a talk of Schatzman's that ended with a brainteaser for the audience to dream on: What phrase does the following represent?

B.A.B.S.

Parsifal studied the problem at bedtime. She dreamed she was in a frigid room. She searched for a means to warm it and found a thermostat—which read zero. Parsifal tried to turn the dial up. As she strained, it barely moved. Finally she got it a couple of degrees higher.

She recorded the dream and told it to me. I recognized the solution in it immediately—but I'd already solved it awake. Parsifal didn't see a reference to the problem. I encouraged her to tell her dream to Schatzman, who, excited, told her yes, exactly— she'd dreamt the solution! Parsifal was still baffled. We both coaxed her to repeat the details about "two degrees" and moving the dial "above zero." Awake, she never solved the puzzle as "two degrees above zero" (we told her eventually, of course). But her dreaming mind sure had!

A similar instance of the Committee's hints going unheeded occurred in Dement's experiment in response to the question "HIJKLMNO: What one word does this sequence represent?" One subject reported: "I had several dreams all of which had *water* somewhere. . . ." The subject proceeded to describe the water imagery in all four dreams: skin diving, heavy rain, hunting sharks, and sailing. He'd already solved the problem to his satis- faction—though incorrectly—before sleep and wrote "alphabet" on the questionnaire without considering that *water* equals H_2O or the letters H to O.[8]

We don't always see answers handed to us awake. This chapter's title probably set you to wondering what word starts and ends with "he," but you may not have seen the answer in the sub- title (go back and reread it). It's obvious now that you know the answer, but you may have missed it initially because, even though you were looking for it, you weren't expecting it *there*. It's easy to overlook answers in our dreams for exactly this reason.

If you're curious to try dreaming on a brainteaser yourself, here are three examples you can try. (Answers appear at the end of the chapter.) These are in approximate order of difficulty. Read the first one at bedtime and try to solve it for ten to fifteen minutes. If you should solve it awake, then go on to the next problem. Follow the rest of the dream incubation instructions in Chapter 7 as closely as possible.

1. Only one word in the English language ends with *mt*— what is it?
2. What occurs once every minute, twice in every moment, but never in a thousand years?
3. One pair of English homonyms (words spelled differently but pronounced the same) have meanings that are exact opposites. What are the words?

It's not necessary to become lucid to solve a puzzle, and it's best to work on simple incubation techniques first. However, if you eventually want to try problem solving via lucidity, here are some steps for that:

• Ask yourself several times each day "Am I dreaming?" Take the question seriously. The effect on your waking consciousness may be interesting as well.
• Identify at least two things that don't work logically in your dreams. Do you have trouble reading? Can you levitate at will? Do light switches fail to change illumination? Or the classic: do you fail to feel pain when you pinch yourself? Use these dream-glitches to test whether you're dreaming. If you do this enough awake, the habit will begin to carry over into sleep.

- As you drift off to sleep at night, remind yourself you want to be lucid in your dreams. Vividly imagine yourself beginning to dream and discovering "Oh! I'm dreaming!"
- If you're doing this for problem solving, also imagine yourself saying "I want to solve the problem" and looking around the dream environment for clues or interviewing a dream character about how they'd approach it.

Sometimes just incubating the problem helps a solution to come in the hypnagogic state. One listener at a talk where I'd offered problem number 1 above told me he half-awoke the next morning and saw the answer (I'm not going to tell you what, of course) repeatedly emblazoned across a screen in front of him.

As in challenges in art, literature, and science, the Committee may solve brainteasers without formal incubation. National Public Radio's Weekend Edition—Sunday show features a segment called "The Puzzle Master." Each week a new brainteaser is offered and people solving the past week's problem are interviewed. The challenge given for the March 12, 2000, show was: "Take the word LIBERALIZATION. Add the letters of SHORTZ and rearrange the result to name part of an airplane. The answer consists of a two-word phrase."

Listener Barbara Tozier solved it: HORIZONTAL STABI-LIZER. Puzzle master Will Shortz asked Ms. Tozier how she figured it out.

"I dreamed it," she replied.

That was all that was said about it on the show, so—being curious—I called Ms. Tozier. She told me she referred to it as a dream because she'd fallen asleep but that the answer simply appeared to her soon after dozing off. "You know how when you're trying to solve a problem at bedtime, once you start dreaming the solution just pops into your mind?" she asked me. Calling on the Committee was second nature to her, but her practice of thinking about it in bed and believing the answer might come is much like formal incubation.

In the conclusion, we'll explore what these dream examples we've been considering tell us about creative problem solving aside from its manifestation in dreams. And we'll see what they say about the nature of dreaming aside from its role in problem solving.

CONCLUSION

$\mathbf{I}$n reading the Committee's more dramatic inventions—especially the whimsical ones of the last chapter—an obvious question arises: Are they for real? We've seen a few people lie or exaggerate—Coleridge about "Kubla Khan," reporters about artist Jencks's nightmare, the myth about Crick and Watson's DNA discovery. But most reports check out—reliable people recount the same story consistently across their lifetimes. Many dreamers are in settings where they would hardly gain by attributing ideas to a dream. During World War II, General George Patton awakened his secretary repeatedly to dictate battle plans he'd just seen in a dream.[1] During the Battle of the Bulge, he carried out a dreamed surprise attack on German troops as they prepared for an offensive against the Allies on Christmas Day. Such successes were welcomed by the military despite—not because of—their source.

A subtler version of the question concerns the accuracy of dream recall. When I talked to mathematician Barry Mazur about the hypnagogically inspired geometry discussed in Chapter 5, he questioned how exact the details were, more than thirty years later. "An anecdote is like a Chinese lacquered box," he suggested. "Each time you tell it, you're adding a coat of lacquer. At the core is something real, but it gets hidden." There's more potential for distortion when people other than the dreamer repeat the story. One of Mazur's students had told me his mathematical inspiration was a dream, while Mazur himself describes it as "browsing" on the verge of sleep. Previous centuries' examples grow more dramatic and lose the corresponding accounts of waking preparation as they're repeated from one writer to another. However, the key idea of the dream invention almost always remains intact.

The creative power of dreaming is regularly discovered anew by ordinary people unaware of its history. A recent exchange on the Internet news group **rec.crafts.textiles.quilting** proceeded as follows:

> It seems whenever I have a problem with a quilt, or am really engrossed with it, I dream the problem out. To my amazement, most of the problems were solved that way.—Rita 4/17/98

> This is interesting. I have never dreamt about solving quilt problems, but when I was in high school and in college (25-plus years apart), I would solve math and chemistry problems in my sleep. I would go to sleep thinking (obsessing) about the problem and would wake up knowing how to solve it. This worked great!—Patty 4/17/98

> All this talk about dreams is too much to keep quiet about. So far, I haven't dreamed about a quilt or chemistry—but when I was eight, I was learning to ride a bike. All day long I got on, fell off—on and off. That night I went to sleep and dreamed I was riding my bicycle. As soon as I woke up, I ran out and just knew I could ride it. I jumped on and didn't fall off all day long.—Vince 4/18/98

The above examples are not as dramatic as those of previous chapters. But they echo several of the themes of this book. The dialogue begins with someone getting visual designs from dreams. Math appears when someone focuses strongly on that. The bicycle example is virtually identical to the one about the old-fashioned high-wheeled bike mentioned in Chapter 7. These patterns have remained remarkably similar across time and across different belief systems.

For centuries, creativity was seen as beyond man, a gift from the gods. If dreams played a role, they were considered divine messages. In the nineteenth century, Goethe and Schiller connected creation with the unconscious. Though still mysterious, the process was now viewed as internally arising rather than externally imposed. Freud's emphasis on dreaming as "the royal road to the unconscious" brought it into this same realm.

Twentieth-century psychologists divide problem solving into four stages: "preparation," "frustration," "inspiration," and "verification." Inspiration cannot be accessed at will, and creativity is most essential here. This is where dreams typically play their role. Any break from concentrated problem solving may allow a misleading assumption to dissipate. But the sleeping mind abandons conventional logic most completely to pursue novel approaches.

How does the Committee do this? Neurology suggests that dreaming is simply the mind thinking in a different biochemical mode. Throughout this emotional, visual, hallucinatory state, we continue to worry about personal, practical, or artistic problems—and occasionally we solve them. Freud wrote of a "dream censor" keeping unacceptable sex and aggression at bay. But as a gatekeeper for novel solutions to problems, the Committee is more liberal than any daytime censor.

As we saw in the first three chapters, visual and narrative ideas are most compatible with dreaming. Logic, music, and math turn up in atypical dreams—those from the verge of sleep or lucid ones. When REM dreams address such topics, they present solutions already complete by the start of the dream. The Committee or Stevenson's "Brownies" have operated beneath the threshold of awareness through our waking hours.

Dreams present most solutions visually (Howe's spearheads, Profet's cartoon bacteria). Verbal ones may employ puns (Stepakoff's "check") or charades (the guillotine to "chop off" letters in Schatzman's brainteaser). But why? Neurologists often say it is because the biochemical state of the brain in sleep favors visual imagery or that visual and motor areas are more active during REM. But that begs the question: *why* does sleeping biochemistry favor it, *why* are the visual centers most active? The best proposed explanation that I've read is in Don Symons's paper "The Stuff That Dreams Aren't Made Of."[2]

Symon's "vigilance hypothesis" argues that sleepers need to monitor their environment—smell smoke, hear intruders, sense temperature changes, and feel pain. It would be maladaptive to hallucinate vividly in most sensory modes. We'd either wake ourselves up in unnecessary panic all the time or we'd have evolved a threshold that caused us to block our real warnings.

Eyes closed, we do not need to monitor our visual environment, and paralyzed we don't need to move—in fact, we shouldn't move until we awaken. So we're free to hallucinate in these modes, Symons says. And, I'd add, this is where the Committee has free reign to express itself, through imagery and motion, for problem solving and other tasks. The amount of attention required to monitor these warning signals is a fraction of what we need to process waking input. Thus the Committee is free to play out ideas that didn't reach consciousness during our busy day—as long as it does so in these modes which evolution has determined don't interfere with our safety.

Personified helpers often do the honors—Einstein for a computer problem, Michael Caine to act out a skit. Some helpers recur across dreams, as with The Man Who Taught Blake Painting, or Horowitz's telescope builder. But it is worth examining *why* the helper format occurs also.

Einstein handing the dreamer a software package sounds like magic. But as we've already seen, our minds perform all manner of calculation beneath the threshold of awareness and perhaps dreams simply personify these solutions. Carl Jung and Fritz Perls built entire dream theories around the premise that all dream characters are split-off parts of ourselves (even those masquerading as people from waking life). Jung and Perls urged their patients to listen to these alternative selves—albeit for emotional wholeness rather than to solve architectural or chemical conundrums.

An abnormal condition that may shed light on this issue is multiple personality disorder. People often wonder how multiple personalities "split," but specialists in the field conceptualize it as the consequence of the self's failure to integrate the fragmented experiences with which we all begin life. Unpredictable childhood trauma encourages several selves to congeal instead of one. A few years ago, I studied dreams of patients with multiple personality disorder. Their "alters," or other personalities, said they could influence the "host" during dreaming. One said, "I show her pictures . . . she sees them best in dreams." Personalities showed up as dream characters giving the host advice or offering information about the past.³ This can be thought of as an exaggeration of normal dreaming—we all project parts of ourselves onto dream characters by a curious mental ventriloquism. One of our nocturnal stage's dummies may have a solution we haven't noticed amid efforts to maintain a unified consciousness.

Gesturing, miming, and the cryptic speech with which solutions appear also occur in other dreams. In two studies I did on people learning to have lucid dreams, they often received these kinds of cues from their dreaming minds.⁴ Dream characters manifested REM movements, pickets appeared with signs declaring, "This World Will End Soon," and one dreamer found a pillow embroidered with the word "Dream." Some would-be lucid dreamers missed their cues, just like those struggling with problem solutions. A stone head told one woman, "This is a dream!" but she merely puzzled about how the sculpture could speak. This isn't intentional game-playing, but rather the best effort by a part of the self with truly odd communication skills. As we've seen earlier, it resembles what has been observed when "split brain" patients tried to communicate from their non-dominant hemisphere.

In the 1970s, Julian Jaynes wrote a remarkable book, *The Origins of Consciousness in the Breakdown of the Bicameral Mind.* He documented the occurrence of voices and visions issuing commands—often to ordinary people and often with good advice. This source of guidance once enjoyed a respected explanation as the voice of the gods, but has been driven underground in modern times. Jaynes asserted that, then and now, the true source of such communications lies within us. Jaynes's one mistake lay in attributing these voices and visions to our right hemisphere. This is too literal an extrapolation from the unusual split-brain patients. Neurologists now understand the sources of most disso-ciation to be more complex. Steinbeck was astute in dubbing it "the *Committee* of Sleep." The subconconscious processes that get their say in our dreams are many and varied—not one cohesive unit. But Jaynes was accurate about the phenomenon itself—and in noting that its most common occurrence is in dreams.

Which brings us to one final issue: Just how unique is this process to dreams? As Jaynes points out, many cultures have a tra-dition of waking visions. And it's more common among the cre-ative. Several visual artists I interviewed were inspired by waking dreamlike imagery. Painter Jim Ann Howard told me of the nighttime dream that led to her *Reunion*. She then recounted the origin of *Trout Dreams* as "walking through a cave and dreaming of fish." Confused, I asked whether she was dreaming or awake. She said, "Awake, but I can dream in either state, so I really don't make much distinction."

An architect friend suggested I contact Morgan Wheelock, the leading Boston landscape architect who has designed many of the lushest city parks and private gardens in the northeast. My friend remembered that his designs came from dreams. However, when I talked to Wheelock, he said "Well, you could call them waking dreams. . . . When I'm looking at a property I'm going to land-scape, I cock my head to the side, breathe a certain way, and the landscape disappears—instead I see it as it could be." It's no won-der my friend remembered this as a dream—that's the only state in which most of us would have such a vivid perception.

A few novelists also have this ability. Stephen King says, "Part of my function as a writer is to dream awake." He describes being completely caught up in a fictional world as he types, and unaware of real objects and events around him.[5] Author James

Hall agrees: "I don't see that the dream state that we have at night is that much different from the dream state that writers learn to put themselves into as they're writing."[6]

So why not do this type of creating when awake? Well, if you can, you should. But I didn't hear these descriptions from creators in most fields—or even from very many painters and writers. Most of us have imagery more tethered to our waking reason. Only about 5 percent of the population has the ability to block out the real world and daydream with hallucinatory vividness. The origin seems to be partially genetic; twins are very similar. It's also partially learned; parents who encourage imaginative play foster this ability in their kids. But the trait is fixed early. A few people learn to harness the latent ability by hypnosis or similar means, but they don't develop it anew as adults. For most of us, dreams remain the only area where imagination runs fully unleashed.

It's common to observe that we spend one-third of our lives asleep—and one-third of *that* in dreaming. In our dream-neglecting culture, two Nobel Prizes resulted from dreams. What might be the potential if we paid as much attention as the cultures we saw in Chapter 8? Dreaming is, above all, a time when the unheard parts of ourselves are allowed to speak—we would do well to listen.

Conclusion

1. The one word in the English language that ends in *-mt*:

    Dreamt. (An especially apt one for the Committee?)

2. What occurs once in every minute, twice in every moment, but never in a thousand years:

    The letter *m*.

3. The pair of English homonyms that have exact opposite meanings:

    Raise (to build up) and *Raze* (to tear down). Another pair that are frequent guesses, but not as perfect opposites, are *whole* and *hole*.

NOTES

CHAPTER I. IN THE GALLERY OF THE NIGHT

1. Alan R. Solomon, *Jasper Johns Exhibit Catalogue* (New York: The Jewish Museum, 1964), 6.

2. Walter Hop, Interview with Jasper Johns, *Artforum*, March 1965, 33.

3. David S. Whitley, "Shamanism and Rock Art in Far Western North America," *Cambridge Archaeological Journal* 2 (1992), 89–113.

4. David Coxhead and Susan Hiller, *Dreams, Visions of the Night* (New York: Avon, 1975), 33.

5. Brian Hill, *Gates of Horn and Ivory: An Anthology of Dreams* (New York: Taplinger, 1968), 59.

6. André Breton, *Manifesto of Surrealism*, in *Manifestos of Surrealism*, translated by Richard Seaver and Helen Land (Ann Arbor: University of Michigan Press, 1969); "omnipotence . . ." 26, "resolution . . ." 14.

7. Salvador Dalí, *Fifty Secrets of Magic Craftsmanship*, translated by Haakon Chevalier (New York: Dover, 1992).

8. Marie-Louise Von Franz, Commentary in *Light from the Darkness: The Paintings of Peter Birkhauser* (Basel, Switzerland: Birkhauser AG, 1980), 80.

9. Columbia Museum of Art, *The Quest of Self-Expression: Painting in Moscow and Leningrad 1965–1990* (New York: 1990).

10. Yve-Alain Bois, *Ellsworth Kelly: The Early Drawings: Kelly's Trouvailles, Findings in France* (Cambridge, Mass.: Harvard Museums, 1999).

11. Stephen LaBerge, *Lucid Dreaming* (New York: Ballantine, 1990).

12. Richard Wilkerson, "Man Against Eternity: The Lucid Dream Wall Art of Epic Dewfall," *Electric Dreams* 4, no. 1 (January 1997).

13. Ernest Hartmann, *The Nightmare: The Psychology and Biology of Terrifying Dreams* (New York: Basic Books, 1984).

14. Paul Laffoley, "The Dream as Initiation," in *The Phenomenology of Revelation* (New York: Kent Fine Art, Inc., 1989), 15–19.

15. J. B. Hawkins, "Pleasant Under Glass," *NC Home*, June 1992.

16. "Buddha House," Episode 601, *Extreme Homes*, House and Garden Television, January 2000.

17. Jean Pierre Jouve and Claude Prevost, *Le Palais ideal du facteur Cheval* (Paris: Covis Prevost Editions du Moniteur, 1981).

18. Alex Gotfryd, *Appointment in Venice* (New York: Doubleday, 1988).

19. Janet Baylis, *"Sleep on It": The Practical Side of Dreaming* (Marina del Rey, Calif.: DeVorss & Co., 1977).

20. National Public Radio 'Victory Garden' program broadcast July 2000.

21. "Gundlach's Clay Works Displayed," *The Oak Ridger*, Oak Ridge, Tenn., 7 May 1998, 11.

Chapter 2. Dreams That Money Can Buy: Filmmaking and Theater

1. Alan Karp, *The Films of Robert Altman* (Metuchen, N.J.: Scarecrow Press, 1981), 119.

2. René Clair, *Reflections on the Cinema,* translated by Vera Trail (London: William Kimber, 1953), 68.

3. George Linden, *Reflections on the Screen* (Belmont, Mass.: Wadsworth, 1970), 173.

4. Vlada Petric, *Film and Dreams* (South Salem, N.Y.: Redgrave Publishing, 1998), 7.

5. J. F. Pagel, C. Kwiatkowski, and K. E. Broyles, "Dream Use in Filmmaking," in *Dreaming: The Journal of the Association for the Study of Dreams* 9, no. 4 (December 1999).

6. British Broadcasting Corporation, *The Definitive Dalí: A Lifetime Retrospective*, video, 1988.

7. Luis Buñuel, *My Last Breath* (London: Jonathan Cape, 1984), 104.

8. Ibid., 92–100.

9. Marsha Kinder, "The Penetrating Dream Style of Ingmar Bergman," in *Film and Dreams: An Approach to Bergman*, edited by V. Petric (South Salem, N.Y.: Redgrave Publishing, 1998), 61.

10. "Conversations with Filmmakers on Dreams," *Dreamworks* 2, no. 1 (Fall 1981), 56.

11. Orson Welles, "Conversations with Filmmakers on Dreams," *Dreamworks* 3, no. 1 (1981), 56.

12. Mark Jordan, "The Stuff of Dreams," *Memphis Flyer*, 28 September 1998.

13. Alan Karp, *The Films of Robert Altman* (Metuchen, N.J.: The Scarecrow Press, 1981). See pages 146–47 for a good description of *Three Women*.

14. Naomi Epel, *Writers Dreaming* (New York: Vintage Books, 1994), 220–21.

15. John Boorman and W. Donohue, "The Burning Question: Is There a Relation Between Dream and Film?" in *Projections 3: Filmmakers on Filmmaking* (New York: Faber & Faber, 1994), 221.

16. D. L. Barrett, "Just How Lucid Are Lucid Dreams: An Empirical Study of Their Cognitive Characteristics," in *Dreaming: The Journal of the Association for the Study of Dreams* 2 (1992), 221–228.

17. K. Kovacs, "Jose Luis Boreau on Movies and Dreams," *Dreamworks* 2, no. 1, (Fall 1981), 64.

18. C. G. Jung, *Analytical Psychology: Its Theory and Practice*, vol. 8 (London: Routledge and Kegan Paul, 1968), 266.

19. Mathew Duda, "Chronology: Ingmar Bergman," in *Film and Dreams: An Approach to Bergman*, edited by V. Petric (South Salem, N.Y.: Redgrave Publishing, 1998), 61.

20. August Strindberg, Introduction to *A Dream Play* (New York and London: Norton, 1973).

21. Jean Cocteau, "The Process of Inspiration," in *The Creative Process*, edited by B. Ghislein (Berkeley: University of California Press, 1952).

22. William Archer, *On Dreams*, edited by T. Besterman (London: Methuen, 1935), 173.

23. R. L. Megroz, *The Dream World* (New York: E. P. Dutton, 1939), 156–57.

CHAPTER 3. THE STATELY PLEASURE DOME: DREAM LITERATURE

1. Mary Wollstonecraft Shelley, *Frankenstein or the Modern Prometheus* (New York: New Orchard Editions, 1986).

2. Synesius, "Dreams Take the Soul to 'The Superior Region,' " in *The World of Dreams*, edited by R. L. Woods (New York: Random House, 1947), 137.

3. J. H. Ingram, *Edgar Allan Poe: His Life, Letters, and Opinions* (New York: AMS Press, 1971), 121.

4. W. B. Yeats, *The Wind Among the Reeds* (London: Elkins Mathews, 1899), 94–95.

5. Katherine Mansfield, journal entry, 10 February 1918, as quoted in B. Inglis, *The Power of Dreams* (London: Grafton, 1987), 10.

6. E. C. Gaskell, *The Life of Charlotte Brontë* (New York: D. Appleton Co., 1857), 243.

7. Walter Scott, *Journal* (New York: Harper & Brothers, 1890), 113.

8. J. Maritain, *The Dream of Descartes* (New York: Philosophical Library, 1944), 14–19.

9. Graham Greene, *Ways of Escape* (London: The Bodley Head, 1980).

10. N. Royle, *The Tiger Garden: A Book of Writer's Dreams* (London: Serpent's Tail, 1996), 217–218.

11. J. Howell, "Just Plain Bill," *High Times*, March 1985, 36.

12. Jack Kerouac, *Book of Dreams* (San Francisco: City Lights Books, 1961).

13. Michael Kreyling, *Author and Agent: Eudora Welty and Diarmuid Russell* (New York: Farrar, Straus & Giroux, 1991), 57.

14. E. B. White, *Letters of E. B. White* (New York: Harper & Row, 1976), 65.

15. Naomi Epel, *Writers Dreaming* (New York: Vintage Books, 1994), 134–36.

16. Ibid., 139–40.

17. Ibid., 214–16.

18. Ibid., 272–73.

19. D. M. Thomas, *Selected Poems* (New York: Viking, 1983), 121.

20. ———, *The Puberty Tree* (London: Bloodaxe Books, 1992).

21. N. Royle, *The Tiger Garden*, 139–40.

22. Epel, *Writers Dreaming,* 9.

23. Ibid., 238.

24. Ibid., 161–62.

25. Ibid., 33, 179–80.

26. Frank McCourt, interviewed in *Poets and Writers*, September/ October 1999.

27. N. Royle, *Tiger Garden*, 45–46.

28. Ernest Hartmann, "We Do Not Dream of the Three R's," *Dreaming* 10, no. 2 (2000), 103–10.

29. K. Mansfield, journal entry (see note 5, above).

30. Epel, *Writers Dreaming*, 94.

31. R. Megroz, *The Dream World: A Survey of the History and Mystery of Dreams* (New York: E. P. Dutton, 1939), 156.

32. N. Royle, *Tiger Garden*, 183–184.

33. Samuel Coleridge, *Kubla Khan* (New York: Dutton, 1933).

34. N. Fruman, *Coleridge: The Damaged Archangel* (London: Allen and Unwin, 1972), 335–38, 551–69.

35. M. Voltaire, "Somnambulists and Dreamers," in *The World of Dreams*, ed. R. Woods (New York: Random House, 1947), 230.

36. A. J. J. Ratcliff, *A History of Dreams: A Brief Account of the Evolution of Dream Theories, with a Chapter on the Dream in Literature* (Boston: Small, Maynard and Co., 1923), 221.

37. Mary Monteith, *A Book of True Dreams* (London: Heath Cranton, Ltd., 1929), 206–7.

38. John Masefield, *The Poems and Plays of John Masefield* (New York: Macmillan, 1922), 767–68.

39. Edwin Diamond, *The Science of Dreams* (London: Eyre and Spottiswoode, 1962).

40. Sir Edmund Gosse, *The Life of Swinburne* (London: Chiswick Press, 1908), 241.

41. Edwin Carpenter, " 'The Creative Process in Dreams' from *The Art of Creation*," in Ralph Woods, ed., *The World of Dreams: An Anthology* (New York: Random House, 1947).

42. J. Mickle (1788), as quoted in Brian Hill, *Cities of Horn and Ivory* (New York: Taplinger, 1967), 46–47.

43. Kenneth Atchity, "The Tom-Otto Plot," *Dreamworks* 4, no. 2 (1984–85), 81–83.

44. Frank Heynick, *Language and Its Disturbance in Dreams* (New York: John Wiley and Sons, 1993), 3.

45. R. P. Warren, to the editor, *Dreamworks* 1 (1981), 128.

46. Marie De Manaceine, *Sleep: Its Physiology, Pathology, Hygiene, and Psychology* (New York: Scribner's, 1897), 314–15.

47. R. L. Stevenson, "A Chapter on Dreams," in *Across the Plains* (Leipzig: Bernhard Tauchnitz, 1892), 211–32. I've changed the third person to first person in these quotes, because out of context the use of third person would be misleading (Stevenson began the essay referring to "a man" and "he," and toward the end acknowledged that he had been referring to himself.)

CHAPTER 4. THE DEVIL PLAYS THE VIOLIN: DREAMS AND MUSIC

1. Barry Miles, *Paul McCartney—Many Years From Now* (New York: Henry Holt, 1997), 201.

2. Chris Salewicz, *McCartney: The Definitive Biography* (New York: St. Martin's Press, 1986), 202.

3. Calvin S. Hall and Robert L. Van De Castle, *Content Analysis of Dreams* (New York: Appleton Century Crofts, 1966).

4. Brewster Ghiselin, *The Creative Process* (Berkeley: University of California Press, 1952), 42–43.

5. G. Johnson, "Music in Dreams," in V. Bass, ed., *Dreams Can Point the Way* (Sugarland, Texas: Miracle House Books, 1984).

6. H. Ellis, *The World of Dreams* (Boston: Houghton Mifflin, 1911), 276–77.

7. Brian Hill, *Gates of Horn and Ivory* (New York: Taplinger, 1968), 69–70.

8. Public Broadcasting System, "Power of Dreams," television documentary, part 2 (1994).

9. "Singing to the Rhythm of Dreams," *Time*, 10 August 1987, 37.

10. Tamela Hultman, interview for Africa News Service with the group's founder, Joseph Shabalala, during a U.S. tour in 1993.

11. Robert Van de Castle, *Our Dreaming Mind* (New York: Ballantine, 1994), 14.

12. National Public Radio, "Weekend Edition," 2 May 1998.

13. *The National Enquirer*, 12 November 1985.

14. Steve Allen, interviewed on *The Merv Griffin Show*, 4 August 1974.

15. Igor Stravinsky and R. Craft, *Expositions and Developments* (Berkeley: University of California Press, 1962), 146.

16. *Gyorgy Ligeti in Conversation with Peter Varai, Josef Hausler, Claude Samuel and Himself* (London: Eulenburg, 1983), 33–34.

17. Mary Monteith, *A Book of True Dreams* (London: Heath Cranton, Ltd., 1929), 34–35.

18. Theodore Levin, liner notes to Huun-Huur-Tu's CD, *Sixty Horses in My Herd* (Shanachie, 1993), translated and paraphrased from Valentina Suzukei, *Tuvan Traditional Musical Instruments*, from oral recitation of Kombu Oorzhak (b. 1917).

19. Hill, *Gates of Horn*, 22–23.

20. H. C. Schonberg, *Horowitz: His Life and Music* (New York: Simon and Schuster, 1992), 171–72.

CHAPTER 5. THE COMMITTEE OF SLEEP WINS A NOBEL PRIZE: DREAMS IN SCIENCE AND MATH

1. All Margie Profet quotes are from a 24 May 1998 telephone interview with the author.

2. A. Toufexis, "A Woman's Best Defense? A Maverick Scientist Contends That Menstruation Protects Against Infection," *Time,* 4 October 1993, 72–73.

3. August Kekulé, "Benzolfest-Rede. Bericht der Deutschen Chemischen Gesellschaft 23 (1890), 1302–11," translated by O. T. Benfy, *Journal of Chemical Education* 35 (1958), 21–23.

4. Eduard Faber, "Dreams and Visions in a Century of Chemistry," in O. T. Benfy, ed., *Kekulé Centennial* (Washington, D.C.: American Chemical Society, 1966).

5. Brian Inglis, *The Power of Dreams* (London: Grafton Books, 1987), 4.

6. A. Sonnet, *Twilight Zone of Dreams* (Philadelphia: Chilton, 1961).

7. W. Dement, *Some Must Watch While Some Must Sleep* (San Francisco: W. H. Freeman & Co., 1972), 98.

8. O. B. Ramsay and A. J. Rocke, "Kekulé's Dreams: Separating the Fiction from the Fact," *Chemistry in Britain* 20 (1984), 1093–94.

9. Elizabeth Agassiz, ed., *Louis Agassiz, His Life and Correspondence* (New York: Houghton, Mifflin & Co., 1885).

10. Otto Loewi, "An Autobiographical Sketch," *Perspectives in Biology and Medicine,* Autumn 1960, as quoted in Edwin Diamond, *The Science of Dreams* (New York: McFadden Books, 1963), 155.

11. Both the Maskelyne and Condorcet stories can be found in Mary Arnold Forster, *Studies in Dreams* (New York: Macmillan, 1921), 83–84.

12. Hilprecht's dreams were published by W. Romaine Newbold in "Subconscious Reasoning," *Proceedings of the Society for Psychical Research* 12, 11–20.

13. Robert Van de Castle, *Our Dreaming Mind* (New York: Ballantine, 1994), 35.

14. Robert Kanigel, *The Man Who Knew Infinity: A Life of the Genius Ramanujan* (New York: Scribner's, 1991), 36.

15. Ibid., 66.

16. Romaine Newbold, "Subconscious Reasoning," *Proceedings of the Society of Psychical Research* 12, 11–20.

17. Forster, *Studies in Dreams,* 83.

18. Stephen LaBerge and Howard Rheingold, *Exploring the World of Lucid Dreaming* (New York: Ballantine, 1990), 178.

19. F. Marton, P. Fensham, and S. Chaiklin, "A Nobel's-Eye View of Scientific Intuition," *International Journal of Science Education* 16 (1994), 457–73, as cited in Guy Claxton, "On Knowing and Not Knowing Why," *The Psychologist,* May 1998, 219–20.

20. Claxton, "On Knowing and Not Knowing Why," *The Psychologist,* May 1998, 217–20.

CHAPTER 6. OF SEWING MACHINES AND OTHER DREAMS: INVENTIONS OF THE COMMITTEE

1. Jason Forsyth, "The Dream Machine," *Success,* October 1990, as quoted in Charles Thompson, *What a Great Idea!* (New York: HarperPerennial, 1992), 208.

2. Hong Sang Dae, *Josun Yuksa Sa* (History of the Enemy) (Seoul, Korea: Hak Yon Chul Pan Sa Publishers, undated), as translated by Fred Jeremy Seligson in a personal communication to the author.

3. Yi Sun-shin, *War Diary of Admiral Yi Sun-shin,* translated by Ha Tae-hung (Korea: Najung i lgi, 1981).

4. William O. Stevens, *The Mystery of Dreams* (London: George Allen, 1950), 34.

5. Ibid.

6. W. H. Moorcroft, *Sleep, Dreaming and Sleep Disorders: An Introduction* (Lanham, Md.: University Press of America, 1989).

7. W. Kaempffert, *A Popular History of American Inventions* (New York: Scribners, 1924), 381–82.

8. N. D. Fagan, ed., *A History of Engineering and Science in the Bell System,* vol. 2 of *National Service in War and Peace (1925–1975)* (Murray Hill, N.J.: Bell Telephone Laboratories, Inc.), 135–48.

9. Author's interview with the late Mildred Hirschberg's daughter, Betty Levy, April 2000.

10. B. M. Kedrov, "On the Question of Scientific Creativity," *Volprosy Psikologii* 3 (1957), 91–113, quoted in Stephen LaBerge, *Lucid Dreaming* (Los Angeles: Tarcher, 1985).

11. Marquis Hervey de Saint-Denys, *Dreams and How to Guide Them,* edited by Morton Schatzman, translated by Nicholas Fry (London: Duckworth, 1982), 92.

12. NBC, *The Secret World of Dreams,* television broadcast, May 1995.

13. Anjali Hazarika, *Daring to Dream: Cultivating Corporate Creativity Through Dreamwork* (New York: Sage, 1998). Hazarika's general approach is outlined in her book, but the two dream examples are from a personal conversation with the author in the fall of 1999.

CHAPTER 7. THE CLAW OF THE PANTHER: DREAMS AND THE BODY

1. Robin Royston, "Illness in Dreams," talk presented at the Thirteenth International Conference of the Association for the Study of Dreams, Berkeley, Calif., 8 June 1996.

2. Aristotle as quoted in S. M. Oberhelman, "Galen on Diagnosis from Dreams," *Journal of the History of Medicine and Allied Sciences* 38 (1985), 37.

3. S. Oberman, "Galen on Diagnosis from Dreams," p. 36–47.

4. Hippocrates, *Dreams,* vol. 4 of *Hippocrates,* translated by William H. Jones (London: Loeb Classical Library, 1931), 438.

5. T. M. Davie, "Comments Upon a Case of Periventricular Epilepsy," *British Medical Journal,* 17 August 1935, 11, 293–29.

6. C. G. Jung, "The Tavistock Lectures," in *The Symbolic Life: The Collected Works,* vol. 18 (Princeton, N.J.: Princeton University Press, 1935), 65–67.

7. Medard Boss, *The Analysis of Dreams* (New York: Philosophical Library, 1958).

8. P. Garfield, *The Healing Power of Dreams* (New York: Simon and Schuster, 1991), 153–54.

9. Oliver Sacks, "Neurological Dreams," in D. Barrett, ed., *Trauma and Dreams* (Cambridge: Harvard University Press, 1996), 212–16.

10. Alan Siegel, *Dreams That Can Change Your Life* (San Francisco: Tarcher, 1992).

11. D. Schneider, *Revolution in the Body-Mind: Forewarning Cancer Dreams and the Bioplasma Concept* (Easthampton, N.Y.: Alexa Press, 1976).

12. Shanee Stepakoff, personal communication with the author.

13. Vasilii Kasatkin, *Theory of Dreams* (Leningrad: Meditsina, 1967), as translated and quoted in Patricia Garfield, *The Healing Power of Dreams* (New York: Simon and Schuster, 1991), 100–33.

14. W. Dick and H. Gris, "Dreams Are Saving Lives," *National Enquirer,* 18 March 1975, 8.

15. Kasatkin, *Theory of Dreams,* as translated and quoted in Garfield, *The Healing Power of Dreams,* 100–33.

16. R. Smith, "Evaluating Dream Function: Emphasizing the Study of Patients with Organic Disease," in R. Haskell, ed., *Cognition and Dream Research,* special issue of *Journal of Mind and Behavior* 7 (1986), 206.

17. Robert Bosnak, "Integration and Ambivalence in Transplants," in

D. Barrett, ed., *Trauma and Dreams* (Cambridge, Mass.: Harvard University Press), 217–30.

18. L. Talamonte, *Forbidden Universe* (New York: Stein & Day), 1975.

19. Ann Faraday, *The Dream Game* (New York: Harper & Row, 1974).

20. Jack Nicklaus, *San Francisco Chronicle*, 27 June 1964.

21. *Sports Illustrated*, 8 April 1974.

22. Rapoport, Ron, *See How She Runs* (Chapel Hill, N.C.: Algonquin, 2000), 206–207.

23. Robert Van de Castle, *Our Dreaming Mind* (New York: Ballantine, 1994); 15.

24. Oliver Sacks, "Neurological Dreams," 214.

25. Peter and Elizabeth Fenwick, *The Hidden Door: Understanding and Controlling Dreams* (New York: Berkeley Books, 1998), 106–7.

26. Daryoush Tavanaiepour and Deirdre Barrett, "Effects of Imagery Rehearsal and Dream Incubation on Championship Swimming," talk presented at the 17th Annual International Conference of the Association for the Study of Dreams, Washington, D.C., 4–8 July 2000.

CHAPTER 8. WHEN GANDHI DREAMED OF RESISTANCE: THE COMMITTEE IN NON-WESTERN CULTURES

1. S. W. Koelle, *Grammar of the Vei Language* (London: Church Missionary House Press, 1853). The simile quote is from page 63.

2. Sylvia Scribner and Michael Cole, *The Psychology of Literacy* (Cambridge, Mass.: Harvard University Press, 1981).

3. Tamela Hultman, Africa News Service interview with Joseph Shabalala during 1993 U.S. tour.

4. Kelly Bulkeley, *Spiritual Dreaming: A Cross-Cultural and Historical Journey* (New York: Paulist Press, 1995), 94.

5. Robert Kanigel, *The Man Who Knew Infinity: A Life of the Genius Ramanujan* (New York: Scribner's, 1991).

6. M. K. Gandhi, *My Autobiography, or My Experiments with Truth,* translated by M. Desai (Ahmedabad, India: Navahvan Publishing, 1957), 337–39.

7. Robert Van de Castle, *Our Dreaming Mind* (New York: Ballantine, 1945), 41.

8. N. MacKenzie, *Dreams and Dreaming* (New York: Vanguard Press, 1965), Chapter 2.

9. R. de Becker, *The Understanding of Dreams and Their Influence on the History of Man* (New York: Hawthorn Books, 1968), 45–47.

10. D. Barrett and J. Behbehani, "Post-traumatic Nightmares in Kuwait Following the Iraqi Invasion." Paper presented at the Twelfth International Conference of the Association for the Study of Dreams, New York, June 1995.

11. *Arizona Highways*, April 1979.

12. Bulkeley, *Spiritual Dreaming*, 87–88.

13. Ibid., 88.

14. Ibid., 90.

Chapter 9. What Word Starts and Ends with "He"? Sleep on a Brainteaser and Wake Up with a Headache

1. M. Schatzman, *New Scientist*, 9 June 1983, 692–93.

2. W. Dement, *Some Must Watch While Some Must Sleep* (San Francisco: W. H. Freeman & Co., 1972), 99–101.

3. Ibid.

4. D. Barrett, "The 'Committee of Sleep': A Study of Dream Incubation

for Problem Solving," *Dreaming: The Journal of the Association for the Study of Dreams* 3 (1993), 115–22.

5. M. Schatzman, *New Scientist*, 25 December 1987, 36–39.

6. ———, *New Scientist*, 11 August 1983, 3–4.

7. Ibid.

8. Dement, *Some Must Watch*, 100.

Conclusion

1. Ladislas Farago, *Patton: Ordeal and Triumph* (New York: Dell, 1965), 354.

2. Donald Symons, "The Stuff That Dreams Aren't Made of," *Cognition* 47 (1993), 181–217.

3. **Rec.crafts.textiles.quilting** at **www.dejanews.com**, 17–18 April 1998.

4. D. L. Barrett, "Dreams in Multiple Personality," in D. Barrett, ed., *Trauma and Dreams* (Cambridge, Mass.: Harvard University Press, 1996); D. L. Barrett, "Just How Lucid Are Lucid Dreams: An Empirical Study Of Their Cognitive Characteristics," *Dreaming: The Journal of the Association for the Study of Dreams* 2 (1992), 221–28; and D. L. Barrett, "Dreaming about Dreamwork," *Dream Network Bulletin*, March 1983, 27–30.

5. Naomi Epel, *Writers Dreaming* (New York: Vintage Books, 1994), 141.

6. Ibid., 110.

ACKNOWLEDGMENTS

I want to thank Andrew Szanton for organizing the writing group to which I belong and for his invaluable advice and painstaking editing as the book evolved. The other members of the group—Tom Land, John Brackett, Jeri Berman, Elizabeth Hale, Joanne Southwell, and Ian Ruderman—all offered generous critique and support. Janna Malamud Smith, Richard Russo, Joe Dixon, Bill Barton, Sharish Korde, and my parents, John and Barbara Barrett, also read portions of the manuscript and suggested valuable changes and additions. Betsy Rapoport, my editor at Crown Publishers/Random House, Stephanie Higgs, her assistant, and my agent, Stuart Krichevsky, were a delight to work with.

The Association for the Study of Dreams, through its annual conferences, Web site, and publications, introduced me to many of the anecdotes and dreamwork techniques presented in this book; the references notes read like its membership roster. Two ASD members' work—Naomi Epel's *Writers Dreaming* and Morton Schatzman's articles on dreams are quoted extensively. Lastly, I want to thank the dreamers—my own interviewees and those through history—who took time to describe their gifts from the Committee so that others may be more attentive to its productions.

Readers wishing to learn more about the Association for the Study of Dreams are encouraged to view their Web site at www.AS Dreams.org or write to them at P.O. Box 1166, Orinda, CA 94563.

INDEX

INDEX

Index

ABOUT THE AUTHOR

DEIRDRE BARRETT, Ph.D., is an assistant professor of psychology at Harvard Medical School. She is the author of the widely acclaimed *The Pregnant Man and Other Cases from A Hypnotherapist's Couch* (Times/Random House, 1998) and editor of the scholarly book, *Trauma and Dreams* (Harvard University Press, 1996). She is former president of the Association for the Study of Dreams, editor-in-chief of the international journal *Dreaming,* and author of dozens of professional articles and chapters on dreams, imagery, and hyponosis.

Dr. Barrett's commentary on dreams has been featured on NBC, The Discovery Channel, and *Voice of America.* She has been interviewed for dream articles in *Life* magazine, *Playboy, Self,* and other national venues. Her own articles have appeared in *Psychology Today* and her film review column, "The Dream Videophile" appears regularly in the magazine *Dream Time.* Dr. Barrett has lectured on dreams at the Smithsonian, at universities across the United States, and in Russia, Kuwait, Israel, England, and Holland. She resides and has her clinical practice in Cambridge, Massachusetts.